NATURAL
MAGICK

First published in 2021 by Leaping Hare Press
an imprint of The Quarto Group.
The Old Brewery, 6 Blundell Street
London, N7 9BH,
United Kingdom
T (0)20 7700 6700
www.QuartoKnows.com

A catalogue record for this book is available from the British Library.

ISBN 978-0-7112-6683-4
Ebook ISBN 978-0-7112-7173-9

10 9 8 7 6 5

Commissioning editor Chloe Murphy
Cover and interior illustrations by Viki Lester of Forensics & Flowers
Design by Georgina Hewitt

Printed in China

The Witch of
the Forest's Guide to

NATURAL
MAGICK

Discover your magick. Connect
with your inner & outer world

LINDSAY SQUIRE

CONTENTS

MY STORY

For as long as I can remember, I've felt a strong pull toward nature and Witchcraft. I loved the magick of the turning of the seasons long before I even knew what The Wheel of the Year was. But it wasn't until I was 22 that these interests turned into a practice and became my way of life.

I began my Witchcraft journey when I began to practice Wicca, where many begin their journey. At the time, I was very much a 'witch in the broom closet,' where I stayed for nearly ten years due to family circumstances that are, thankfully, no longer an issue. I like to call that my former life, but it really shaped my early years in the Craft. Like many people in the broom closet, I had to get creative, and it's surprising how many tricks you pick up over the years that allow you to practice your Craft under the radar.

Social media played a huge part on my Witchcraft journey, as it gave me a place to express myself, talk to like-minded people and learn about the Craft in a discreet way. I started my Instagram account @thewitchoftheforest in 2012 to create a safe, anonymous space for me to explore Witchcraft. I didn't want to use my real name, so I adopted the name The Witch of the Forest. As an Earth sign (I'm a stubborn Taurus), I get so much of my grounding and balance from being outside and connecting to nature, especially in woods and forests. I could picture myself as an old woman, living in a little house in the middle of a beautiful pine forest, growing my own food and herbs, mixing potions and living the simple life. I really felt The Witch of the Forest perfectly captured the essence of my Craft at the time, and it still resonates with me so much now.

Over the years, my Instagram account has helped me to meet so many wonderful people and make some amazing friends. I truly feel blessed to have them all in my life, as each one has had a positive impact upon my Craft and has helped me grow and evolve. I never thought it would one day provide a space that would enable me to share my knowledge and give practical guidance to other Witches. I want to say thank you, from the bottom of my heart, to everyone who has helped me along the way, and to you, reading this book right now. I truly am so thankful for your presence and for all your support and help.

I hope this book helps you along your journey and helps you connect with yourself and the natural world on a deeper level. As Witches, we all walk very different paths, but my wish is that this book will help you discover the path that is right for you. There is no wrong way or right way to practice Witchcraft, just your way. Remember, if you are looking for the right way to go in the Craft, we are all our own best teacher.

I am honored that I can walk with you on your path as you have been there on mine.

Lindsay

THINGS TO KNOW BEFORE
you embark on your journey through this book:

EVERYBODY'S PATH & PRACTICE IS DIFFERENT

When I began my Craft, my practice was influenced by East Anglian Witchcraft and later Cornish traditional Witchcraft. After practicing Wicca in the broom closet for a few years, my Craft then evolved into the more traditional practice it is today, as I felt connected to how it lent equal value to light/dark, left/right, masculine/feminine and the known/unknown.

Yet when I first started out in the Craft, having a label for my Craft felt important to help me figure out who I was. I felt I needed to have a specific identity and the order that this identity brought. As I developed though, I started to feel that labels were restrictive. I discovered that by focusing more on one area of the Craft in order to fulfill and embody a specific identity, I neglected a lot of my other skills and it made my Craft feel unbalanced. I needed to learn to embrace the Witch I was, and that meant accepting that although I didn't fall into any specific type of Witchcraft, it didn't mean I wasn't a 'real' Witch.

Whoever you are and however you came to the Craft, you don't need to label your practice. Don't worry about how you categorize your Craft.

It's more important to find the path that feels right and is authentic to you.

YOU DON'T NEED TO BE A HEREDITARY WITCH TO PRACTICE POWERFULLY

There is often a misconception that being a hereditary Witch somehow makes your Craft more valid compared to someone (like me) who is walking their own path as the first Witch in their family. But as beautiful as it is to come from a long line of Witches, with all the family history, traditions and practices associated with it, it is not necessary to become a Witch.

YOU CAN PRACTICE ALONE OR AS PART OF A COMMUNITY

Being a solitary practitioner or a Witch initiated into a coven makes you an equally authentic Witch. The kind of Witch you become is completely in your own hands and will be shaped by your commitment to researching, learning, practicing and honoring Witchcraft.

It can feel overwhelming to begin your Witchcraft journey alone. There is so much to learn and it's not always easy to find accurate information or know where to start. But this book will help you navigate and find the right path for you. It can act as your starting point at the beginning of your journey, or as a place to check in with and re-center your practice further down the line. Either way, I have filled it with resources I wish I had had when I began my own journey.

YOUR CRAFT DOESN'T HAVE TO COST A FORTUNE

An important point all Witches, not just those at the start of their journey, should know is that your practice doesn't have to cost a fortune. Social media can give the impression that to be a Witch, you must wear all black, have a cauldron, a fully stocked herb cupboard, incense, every color of candle and every crystal, all of which can cost a small fortune. But being a Witch is so much more than the kind of tools you use or clothes you wear, and having these things doesn't mean your magick will be any stronger or your spells more successful. Whether you enjoy collecting and using these items or your toolkit is more minimalist, your practice will be just as powerful either way. It's the strength, power, and focus of your intention that matters.

WHETHER YOU'RE A WITCH IN THE BROOM CLOSET OR AN OUT-AND-PROUD WITCH IN PROGRESS, THIS BOOK IS FOR YOU

I understand how hard it is to have to hide the magickal part of yourself from the people around you. This is why, as my Craft has grown, I have wanted to help other Witches who don't have the option to come out of the broom closet to practice their Craft in a way that is both fulfilling and subtle. For example, there are so many ways to celebrate the Sabbats, honor the cycles of the Moon and perform magick in a way that isn't obvious to the untrained eye.

HAVE FUN & MAKE YOUR OWN MAGICK

It's easy to get caught up in the aesthetic Witchcraft on social media, but Witchcraft is raw and is not always so neat and tidy. Give yourself permission to have fun and find your own kind of magick and authentic style. Play, adapt and find what works for you. Feel free to take any spells or recipes in this book as guidelines, and make them your own by adding items or substituting ingredients to suit your needs and intentions. Make this magick your own!

AND REMEMBER, A WITCH NEVER STOPS LEARNING

As you discover more about the Craft, you will also discover so much about yourself as you learn to connect with yourself on a deeper level. Magick is a grounding form of nourishment that connects us to the natural world, and to be a Witch is to be aligned and harmonized with the natural world and the elements.

Just like nature, we too are ever-changing and growing. Be dedicated to your own growth and be actively committed to lifelong learning. A Witch's learning is never complete, regardless of how long they have been in the Craft!

1
GETTING
STARTED

Starting your Witchcraft journey, however magickal it may feel, can be overwhelming. Where do you start? What tools do you need? What are the basics you need to know? The list of questions in your mind is probably a long one. And that's completely normal!

When I began to practice Witchcraft, I remember feeling lost, and in the days before social media, it was hard to find information as easily as we can now. This chapter will start to answer some of these questions, and sets out some of the central things about the Craft I wish I had known when I started my journey.

Let's get started!

RESEARCH
Topics

When it comes to starting your Witchcraft practice, the value of undertaking your own research and spending time reading and learning can't be underestimated. If you are a solitary Witch, using your own initiative to learn is how you'll start to build a foundation of knowledge on which your Craft can grow and develop.

I have found in my practice that the only way to make the beginning of my journey feel less overwhelming is to start! You must start somewhere, so pick a topic that really interests you and go from there. It might be tempting to think you need to read anything and everything about Witchcraft at first, but this can add to the feeling of being overwhelmed, so don't be afraid to be selective at first and follow your own particular interests.

If you read something about a practice you don't like or feel comfortable with, move on. Your studies are there to help you build up a better sense of the kind of Witch you are and to help you walk the path that feels right to you. You will probably find that one topic flows into another and your studies will start to take on a life of their own. The hardest part is just starting.

There is no right or wrong way to approach your own learning in terms of the topics you choose to study and in what order. The most important thing is that you are committed to your own growth not only as a Witch, but on a personal level too. It doesn't matter how quickly your studies progress, as long as you are committed to them.

Regardless of how long they have been in the Craft, no Witch knows everything. It is a lifelong journey. A special kind of magick takes place when you realize that the purpose of your journey as a Witch is to continue growing, evolving, and deepening your connection with yourself, your intuition, and with the power of nature, no matter how knowledgeable or advanced you may become.

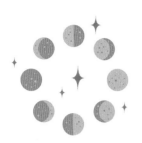

The history of
Witchcraft

Moon phases
and cycles

Types of Witches
and traditions

Types of spells

TOPICS TO
RESEARCH

Color magick

Crystals and their
magickal properties

Methods of divination

The elements

Herbs and
magickal properties

PAGANISM

Paganism is an umbrella term
for all nature-based religions.

Pagans honor ancient deities,
usually the Goddess as the
Moon and the God as the Sun.

WICCA

Wicca is a brand of Paganism and
is called a Neopagan religion.

Wicca is also focused on living
life in tune with nature and
honoring ancient deities.

WITCHCRAFT

Witchcraft is a practice and
not a religion.

Witchcraft is an umbrella
term for those who practice
magickal workings.

PAGANISM, WICCA *& Witchcraft*

Used frequently in books and on social media, often interchangeably, Paganism, Wicca, and Witchcraft are terms that can become really confusing. It can also be hard to gauge where to place yourself and your own beliefs and what you identify as. There are so many "types" of Witches (green, traditional, gray, and so on) but they all fall beneath one (or often more) of the three main umbrella terms of Paganism, Wicca, and Witchcraft.

In broad terms, Paganism is any religion, usually in Western Europe, that is not one of the three Abrahamic religions—Judaism, Christianity, and Islam. More specifically, Paganism is the term used to describe those who follow a nature- or Earth-based folk religion and honor ancient deities. It's based on the rhythms and cycles of the natural world, including the seasons and the phases of the Moon. Pagans believe in both a God and a Goddess (although some Pagans honor more than just one of each), with an emphasis on balance. Under the umbrella that is Paganism, there is a vast number of different traditions such as Wicca, Shamanism, Druidry, and Asatru, and although they may be called different names, they are all considered to be branches of Paganism.

A Wiccan is a person who is a Pagan and a practitioner of Witchcraft, so is also Witch (regardless of gender). Wicca is a Neopagan religion, where the Goddess is the Moon and the God is the Sun; some branches of Wicca honor more deities. This is a personal choice that allows you to find your own path and do what feels right for you. All Wiccans follow the Wheel of the Year (see Chapter 2) and have the Wiccan Rede as a moral system for their practices. The Rede is simple and states, "An ye harm none, do as you will", (Do as you wish, as long as it doesn't harm anyone), which are the fundamentals of the Wiccan religion.

Witchcraft is a practice and not a religion, which is why it's called a "craft". It involves the practice of magickal skills (like spell-work and rituals) that are guided by your own moral code and ethics. A Witch can follow many paths and it is up to the individual to forge their own path. It's important to note that all Wiccans are Witches and Pagans, but not all Witches are Wiccan and Pagan. Not all Witches are religious and believe in any deities, but rather they follow and honor the rhythms of nature.

CAULDRON
Metal pot used to burn or hold spell ingredients—symbolizes the divine feminine.

BOLINE
A white-handled knife used to cut herbs and carve candles.

CANDLES
Used in spells, rituals, and as a meditation aid, candles are the most common Witchcraft tool.

USEFUL WITCHCRAFT TOOLS

HERBS SPICES & RESINS
Use for spells, rituals and potions, oils, and infusions.

MORTAR & PESTLE
The traditional way to grind up herbs, spices, and resins.

INCENSE
Represents the four elements. Use for rituals and spells, as energy is released when burned.

BESOM
A broom used for cleansing and sweeping away negative energy.

USEFUL
Witchcraft Tools

When it comes to tools of the Craft, what you choose to use is a personal choice. Most of the tools in my Craft are there to perform a practical use, so I've chosen the items that I use the most as a rough guide. Some of them are inexpensive so are also great for Witches on a budget. If you opt not to use some of them, but use others, remember it is your choice and there is no right or wrong way, just your way. Use the tools that feel right to you.

The cauldron will always be synonymous with Witchcraft and it's certainly a useful tool to own. Traditionally, a cauldron is a cast iron/metal pot with a handle and lid, used for cooking over a fire. In Witchcraft, it has a myriad of uses. It can be used to burn items for magickal workings and hold spell ingredients. Filling up a cauldron and adding a drop of black food coloring makes the perfect surface for scrying (see page 168) too!

Candle magick is one of the most common forms of Witchcraft. It's one of the least expensive items too, as all you need is the strength of your intention and something to light them with. When it comes to green Witchcraft, a mortar and pestle is a very useful tool to have. Although sometimes a bit heavy on the hand and wrist, it's a traditional way to grind up herbs, spices, and resins. A good tip is to focus your intentions for your working as you grind your ingredients, to amplify the energy they bring.

Incense is another inexpensive tool at a Witch's disposal, whether it be in cone, stick, or loose form. It represents the four elements: the smoke wafts through the air, which is created by fire; it uses materials that have been grown and made by the earth; and is formed by using water. Burning incense helps to create the right atmosphere for your workings and helps to focus your attentions on the purpose of a spell/ritual.

A boline (or bolline) is traditionally a single-bladed, white handled ritual knife. It's used for carving things like symbols into candles during a spell or ritual, as well as for cutting magickal ties. It is useful because not only does a boline fulfill a ritualistic role, but it has many practical uses too. It can also be used for trimming plants and cutting up herbs, string, and ribbons.

A besom is a long-handled broom that can be made by tying twigs to a thin piece of willow wood with string or straw. It is commonly used to sweep away negative energy.

HOUSEHOLD
Tool Alternatives

As good as it might be to have a cauldron or a mortar and pestle, getting hold of these items can be difficult, especially if you're on a budget or are in the broom closet. But there's good news! You don't actually need any of these tools to practice the Craft. They are good to have but not essential. In fact, you probably have things in your house that can be perfect alternatives to many common Witchcraft tools! Just make sure that you thoroughly cleanse any items before you use them. You will find more information on exactly how to cleanse on page 32.

A cauldron can be replaced by something like a saucepan, a slow cooker (crockpot) or any kind of heatproof dish. These can be used for burning spell ingredients, burning candles, and even making magickal food.

A boline is easily made from any kind of kitchen knife, just as long as the blade is sharp enough to cut things like herbs and carve candles.

A mortar and pestle is a must for all green Witches, but there are a few household alternatives. A coffee grinder or blender can do the job just as well, and if you don't have a grinder, using a rolling pin and kitchen cloth works too. Place the ingredients in the cloth and wrap them up, then gently use the rolling pin to break up the ingredients.

A wand—a thin, light rod used to channel and direct energy—can be made of any wood. Go out and forage for a branch that calls to you, then carefully whittle it down and even carve meaningful symbols into the wood.

A besom can be replaced with a vacuum cleaner, or even a dustpan and brush. It's the action of sweeping away negative energy that matters, not the method you chose to do it with.

Divination is a big part of a Witch's Craft, but you can easily carve your own sigils (which you will learn about in Chapter 6) into salt dough instead of wood, chalk, or stone. To make salt dough, use 2 cups of plain flour, 1 cup of salt and up to 1 cup of water. Knead the mixture into a dough and separate into 24 small balls. Make them into disc shapes and bake in the oven at 250°F/120°C/Gas ½ for 3 hours. Decorate by carving when cool, being sure to focus your attentions on the purpose of a spell/ritual.

HOUSEHOLD TOOL ALTERNATIVES

COFFEE GRINDER
A grinder can often replace a a mortar and pestle.

KITCHEN KNIFE
A staple of every kitchen, a kitchen knife can be used as a boline.

COOKING POT
Use a crockpot or suacepan as you would a couldron.

DUST PAN AND BRUSH
Visualize sweeping away negative energy like a besom using a dust pan and brush.

TREE BRANCH
Search the ground for a branch of wood to fashion into a wand.

SALT DOUGH SIGILS
Make your own set of sigils using salt dough.

ALL THE POWER IS
ALREADY INSIDE YOU

INTENT & *Witchcraft*

Intent plays a central role in Witchcraft: it's what helps to drive your magick forward. An intent is deciding what you want the outcome of your workings to be and then communicating that to the universe (or whatever power you work with) as clearly and precisely as possible.

It's best to be as specific as you can when telling the higher force you are working with (whether that's the universe, a deity, your higher self or another power) exactly what you want, as being clear helps to ensure that your workings don't manifest any unwanted energies. Intention is where a lot of your power for your works and comes from. This is a skill you will develop as you practice more, and the wonderful thing about intention is that all the power is already inside you: it's not a tool you have to purchase to activate and use, but a skill you can hone without the use of many accompanying materials.

Intent is not the only important thing you need to harness to ensure successful spells—you must harness your inner energy and the energy around you, too. Energy is "raised" as a result of our magickal workings, the ingredients we use, and our words and actions. Intention acts as a kind of filter for all this energy and it works to guide it into the direction of your desired outcome. Intention strengthens and concentrates the energy you raise, which increases the efficacy and speed of your workings. As you practice your Craft, you will learn to hone and strengthen your intent, and work with raising your energy.

When you set intentions, it's also crucial to ensure you do your share of the work to drive the process forward. You must make the necessary changes to your behavior so you can align your actions with your intentions and values, and meet the power you are working with halfway. For example, if you want to manifest a new job, you must do your share of the work to help bring this result about, such as keeping your CV up to date and actively looking for and applying for the jobs you want.

The changes you make to your behavior should be mundane as well as magickal. Learning to balance intent, energy, and action will help you develop a stronger understanding of how magick works, and will help you to become completely invested in the process of creating the change you need. The more understanding of magick you can acquire through practice, the more effective a Witch you will grow to become.

EARTH | NORTH

Green/Brown | Winter Solstice

Capricorn • Taurus • Virgo

Apple, comfrey, cypress, fern, all grains, all grasses, honeysuckle, ivy, mugwort, oak, primrose, rhubarb, vervain

WATER | WEST

Blue | Autumn Equinox

Cancer • Scorpio • Pisces

Chamomile, cardamom, heather, jasmine, lemon, lilac, lily, seaweed sandalwood, rose, vanilla

AIR | EAST

Yellow | Spring Equinox

Aquarius • Gemini • Libra

Citron peel, frankincense, bergamot, lavender, lemon verbena, lemongrass, marjoram, mint, star anise, yarrow

FIRE | SOUTH

Red/Orange | Summer Solstice

Sagittarius • Leo • Aries

Allspice, basil, bay-laurel, cinnamon, cloves, cilantro, dill, fennel, garlic, nettles, nutmeg, peppermint, rosemary

THE
Elements

Nature is the foundation of Witchcraft, and the four elements play a central role in this. For thousands of years, alchemists have worked with the four elements; the building blocks of the universe. Earth, Air, Fire and Water play an integral part in the cycle of birth, death, and rebirth happening all around us in natural world. On the opposite page, I have included a non-exhaustive list of some of the herbs best associated with each element.

Elemental magick is about harnessing one or more of the elements to use their power in your workings. Each of the elements has a specific kind of spiritual energy and can be invoked as part of a ritual or spell to harness these energies. This will add power to your workings. It's a good type of magick to start with as it involves basic ingredients such as soil for Earth, a candle for Fire, a feather for Air, and a cup of water. As my own Craft is not deity or religion based, working with the elements feels very natural. Learning to connect with them and balance their forces in your life not only enriches your Craft, but helps you to connect with yourself and nature on a deeper level.

Many Witches, not just Neopagans (Wiccans), who work with the rhythms of nature, work with the elements in their Craft. Elemental magick is the practice of raising and using the energy of one or more of the elements in your workings. Energy is the foundation of all elemental magick and it's about tapping into this energy and moving and manipulating it toward your own intentions.

To get in touch with the elements, return to nature. Go outside and feel, observe, or touch the solid earth. Feel its energy surging through you and expand your senses so you take in the whole picture, including its smell, sight, sound and feel.

Connect with the air by inhaling deeply, filling your lungs with the invisible element that is fundamental to human life. Feel the relaxing or revitalizing presence of water—visit a lake or river, or fill up a bowl with water so you can feel its power to purify and cleanse.

To connect with the less-present but highly energetic element of fire, light a candle and focus on the flame, feel the warmth, the power, and the strength of its energy. Or, simply close your eyes and take a moment to feel the warmth of the Sun on your skin.

Nature has the power to bring about a greater sense of balance and wellbeing to our lives and connecting with the elements is a simple way to connect with nature and the wider universe. Elemental magick is an accessible form of magick for Witches at all levels and abilities, regardless of where you are on your journey.

GRIMOIRES &
Book of Shadows

It's common practice for Witches to keep a record of their Craft. How you do this is purely a personal choice, and it's about finding out what is best for you. In general terms, Witches keep two main types of magickal records: a Grimoire and a Book of Shadows.

A Grimoire is like a magickal textbook that contains information such as step-by-step instructions for spells and rituals, as well as entries about herbs and crystals and how to prepare magickal items like a talisman (an object that brings good luck). It doesn't contain any personal information about your Craft, just all the magickal research you have undertaken.

A Book of Shadows is a different kind of book. It generally contains all the personal aspects of your workings and Craft, and many Witches opt to keep this as a personal record not meant to be seen by others.

Common things to include in a Grimoire or Book of Shadows include:

☾ A lunar diary
☾ A dream diary
☾ Your natal chart
☾ Successful spells you have tried
☾ Rituals
☾ Recipes
☾ Crystal meanings
☾ Magickal correspondences
☾ Tarot meanings

Whether you keep your Grimoire or Book of Shadows to yourself or choose to show it to others, there is no right or wrong way. Some Witches (myself included) keep a book that is a blend of both a Grimoire and a Book of Shadows, but again, this should be based on what feels right for you.

Witches often pass their Grimoires and Books of Shadows on to the next generation of Witches. So whether you are the first Witch in your family or part of a hereditary line, passing on your books helps to keep your magick alive in order to guide and teach others.

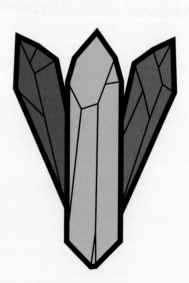

A Grimoire is a magickal textbook that gives information on spells, rituals, and other workings. It contains general magickal knowledge and doesn't often contain personal information. A Book of Shadows contains personal magickal information, generally for your eyes only. It contains entries about your dreams, your personal thoughts, and experiences.

SETTING UP
Your Altar

Altars can be created for a myriad of purposes. Some altars are made to honor a specific deity, while others are working altars where a Witch performs their spells and rituals. Others can be a mixture of the two. Your altar can be as ornate or as plain, as large or as small as you desire. It can also be created wherever you want, and you can have more than one, if you wanted to have separate altar for workings and, say, an ancestor altar.

How you create your altar and what it looks like is down to you. There really aren't any rules to follow—your altar is a representation of your Craft and it should be fit for whatever purpose you want it for.

Ancestor altars are not only for Samhain (see page 36). It's a common practice for many Witches to have a space put aside somewhere to honor their ancestors. This altar could include old pictures, personal items owned by the departed as well as offerings of their favorite food and drinks.

When choosing what you put on your altar, a good rule of thumb is to make sure every piece serves your Craft and spirituality in one way or another. As you evolve on your spiritual journey, you will probably find that your altar will develop as you do and will reflect how you are growing as both a Witch and on a personal level. Like your Grimoire and/or Book of Shadows, you don't have to share pictures of your altar with anyone if you feel uncomfortable and want to keep it for your eyes and Craft only. Equally, if you feel happy and want to share your altar with others, then that's also fine! It's your personal magickal space and it's completely up to you whether you choose to share it.

Remember that you don't have to share any part of your Craft if it makes you feel uncomfortable. Many Witches on social media share aspects of their Craft, such as pictures of their altars and workings, but this doesn't mean you should feel pressured to do the same if it's not the way you want to go. There is not one aspect of your Craft you must share, regardless of the trends on social media, so don't feel you have to go with the flow.

SETTING UP YOUR ALTAR

1. Candles   2. Incense   3. Mortar and pestle   4. Chalice   5. Grimoire/Book of Shadows
6. Representations of deities   7. Offering bowl   8. Cauldron   9. Representations of the elements
10. Gifts from nature: crystals, stones, leaves, earth, flowers, shells   11. Wand   12. Altar cloth

ECO WITCHCRAFT

Grow your own herbs

Don't bury
non-biodegradable materials

Opt for secondhand books

Avoid "one use" plastic items
and find greener alternatives

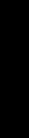

Buy herbs in bulk

Buy ethically sourced crsystals
and herbs

Re-use and repurpose items like
jars and bottles

Dispose of spell remnants
thoughtfully after your workings

Forage for spell items but only
take what you need

Collect your own water for
your craft

ECO
Witchcraft

When we practice our Craft, it's important to make sure it doesn't have a negative effect on the environment. There are lots of little tips and tricks to help make your practice greener. The actions we take can not only protect the planet but help to add energy to your magick because it brings you into greater alignment with the forces of nature.

It's important we have a good relationship with the natural world if we want to raise and use its energy; it's counterproductive to harm the very power you want to work with. Through the choices we make in our Craft, we can have a positive impact on our environment, and the more we do so can help us to connect with nature on a deeper level.

There are more obvious ways you can make your Craft a little greener, such as repurposing and recycling items like glass jars and bottles and avoiding single-use plastics. Other methods include collecting your own rainwater for your workings and being careful not to bury non-biodegradable items such as candle wax.

One of the big ways you can have a positive impact on the environment is to make sure you know the origins of any items you purchase, such as crystals, essential oils, incense, and herbs. Unfortunately, the global trade for these products has got a dark side. Many larger suppliers spray their herbs with chemicals or add synthetic ingredients to essential oils. The over-harvesting of sandalwood has damaged so much of the ecosystem in Australia and India, and the crystal-mining industry is also tainted by conflict: crystals are not a renewable resource and there are big issues surrounding sustainability as well issues of underage labour and exploitation. It's good to know where the items you buy come from so you can make an informed choice.

When it comes to herbs, grow some yourself! It is the greenest way to get the herbs you want for your workings and rosemary, thyme, basil, lemongrass, and mint are easy to grow both outside and inside in plant pots. Foraging is another great option and you might be surprised about which herbs grow naturally around your area. Just be sure to only take what you need rather than plundering what is available to you. It's a great way to learn more about herbs at the same time.

CONSCIOUS *Witchcraft*

Just as it's good to have more awareness about environmental issues connected to your Craft, it's also important to have an awareness about the origins of our practices. We all try to have the best intentions but it's very important to stop and evaluate our practices and have an open mind so we can learn where they first came from and how our practices may affect others.

In recent years, it has become a trend to burn white sage. This practice has entered the mainstream consciousness and now white sage can be bought easily online and in many New Age shops. This practice, where white sage is burned and then the smoke is fanned around the room with a feather, is widely known as 'Smudging'. The problem is that smudging is part of a much larger sacred ceremony, performed by Indigenous people.

Terminology is important. Smudging is regularly taken out of context to mean just burning white sage to cleanse a person or room, when this is only a small part of the traditional Indigenous ceremony of purification. Out of respect for the Indigenous community, many people refrain from using the term 'Smudging' and the use of white sage, instead opting for the term 'smoke cleansing' and burning other herbs more native to them like rosemary, lavender, and juniper.

The same can be said for Palo Santo, which is considered sacred by Indigenous people and often used in the smudging ceremony. While its hallowed status among Indigenous people has become more widely known, there are also huge issues of sustainability too. Contrary to popular belief, the Palo Santo tree is not endangered, but its natural habitat is, and overharvesting has decimated the tropical dry forests where it grows in South America. Ethically sourced Palo Santo is only available where the wood naturally falls from the tree and is dried. Even so, it should not be used as part of a smudging ceremony unless you are an indigenous person.

There are many alternatives to Palo Santo; vervain, yarrow, and mugwort for example, are great for smoke cleansing. But if you decide you still want to use Palo Santo or white sage, make sure you buy them from an Indigenous, sustainable smaller business. Big brands are more likely to be involved in overharvesting, and if you are going to use these materials, it's good to be able to support the livelihoods of the Indigenous communities, and understand more about where the spiritual practices we know them for today came from.

CLEANSING HERB ALTERNATIVES

4. 5.

3. 6.

2. 7.

1. 8.

1. Cinnamon - Psychic abilities, adds energy   2. Peppermint - Renewal, Rest
3. Lemongrass - Energising, Psychic abilites   4. Juniper - Regeneration, Protective
5. Lavender - Healing, Calming   6. Rosemary - Healing, Protection
7. Bay Leaves - Prosperity, Protection   8. Cedar - Protection, Longevity

CLEANSING

Cleansing is the act of removing any negative energies from a person, place, or object. Many Witches regularly cleanse their living space so they so they can create a peaceful and balanced environment to live and practice their magick in. It's also very useful cleanse yourself and your tools before casting a spell or undertaking a ritual to create a balanced energy and the right environment for your workings. Cleansing your tools also ensures there are no unwanted energies attached to them which could affect the energy and outcome of your workings.

When it comes to burning herbs for cleansing purposes, although white sage is often the first herb that comes to mind, with all the cultural and sustainability issues, you might want to opt for other forms of cleansing. There are lots of alternative herbs with purifying and cleansing properties, so you can pick one that is in line with your intention.

Cleansing doesn't just involve herbs. There are various other methods, many of which require few or no tools, so are great for the thrifty Witch! Methods include visualization and the use of the light of a white candle. To visalize, sit comfortably and hold the item you want to cleanse and visualize a bright white light that hovers over the item, then pours into it, washing away any negative energy on and inside the item.

Using sound can also clear the energy of a space, as it helps to move away stagnant energy and raise the vibrations of the area that the sound is in, helping the energy that isn't in resonance with the vibrations to move on out.

Other methods of cleansing without herbs include ritual baths, using a besom to 'sweep' away any negative energy, water cleansing, burying the object associated with negative energy in the soil for 12 to 24 hours, or putting the object into the light of the sun or moon, depending on your intent. Sunlight is associated with action and energy, while moonlight is connected to cleansing and charging. The phase of the moon is also important: be sure to choose the phase that aligns with your intentions so you can harness the exact kind of energy you are trying to raise. Many Witches regularly cleanse their living space so they can create a peaceful and balanced environment to live in.

Sound vibrations: sounds are vibratory and purify a space of negativity
Visualization: visualizing a white light growing will cleanse and purify your space
Flower water: add petals to hot water. and let the steam cleanse your space
White light: use a white candle's light to drive away negativity
Sprays: fill a spray bottle with charged water and mist your space with it
Essential oils: use a diffuser and a cleansing essential oil like lavender

YULE
Winter Solstice

SAMHAIN
All Hallows Eve

IMBOLC
Candle Mass

MABON
Austumn Equinox

OSTARA
Spring Equinox

LAMMAS
Loaf Mass

BELTANE
May Eve

Summer Solstice
LITHA

2

THE WHEEL OF THE YEAR

This chapter will introduce each of the eight Sabbats—Neopagan religious festivals commemorating phases of the changing seasons. It will also include a tarot spread for each, and my favorite correspondences to work with during each one. Correspondences are tables of individual tools and items such as crystals, herbs, colors, and deities that are grouped together, because they share similar magickal properties. They are very useful when planning and constructing any kind of spell or ritual.

Celebrating the Sabbats helps us to align ourselves with Mother Nature as we observe the earthly and celestial cycles. The Sabbats correspond to the movements of the Sun and stars and the changing of the seasons in the natural world. They are pre-Christian customs related mostly the Celtic agricultural festivals, which is where they get their names. It's a way to mark the passage of time, because the Wheel never stops turning.

Not every Witch celebrates all the Sabbats. To honor the turning of the wheel, some observe Samhain, some only celebrate the Solstices, while some choose to follow the changing of the seasons as they experience them. There isn't a right or wrong way to observe the Sabbats and it's always best to follow the path that feels right to you.

THE MEANING OF
Samhain & Tarot Spread

✧✧✧

SYMBOLIZES: Death, ancestors, honor, the thinning Veil, Witches New Year, spirits and the spirit world, change, wisdom

Samhain (pronounced "Sow-en") is a Celtic Sabbat celebrated on October 31 in the Northern Hemisphere and on May 1 in the Southern Hemisphere. It is the first of the four cross-quarter and fire festivals, which mark the four midpoints on the Wheel of the Year between the Spring and Autumn Equinoxes and the Summer and Winter Solstices. Samhain marked summer's end on old Celtic farming calendars. A Greater Sabbat, it is the start of the Witch's new year, and the end of the third and final harvest.

Each Sabbat is associated with a different phase of life for the God and Goddess. This is more of a Neopagan and Pagan belief system and does not need to be part of your Sabbat celebrations as a Witch if it doesn't feel right for you; you can still celebrate the turning of the Wheel through your connection with nature, the way the seasons change around you and the natural passing of time of the Earth.

On this Sabbat, the God of summer, represented by the Sun, dies, signifying the coming of winter as we enter the dark half of the year. The death of the God has a direct consequence on the natural world, and causes the leaves on the trees to fall as he retreats into the shadows before he can be reborn at Yule.

Many Pagan religions, including Wicca, honor the Triple Goddess in her individual aspects of Mother/Maiden/Crone. Each aspect aligns with a different phase of the Moon and charts the three main life phases of the Goddess, which reflect the human experience, regardless of gender, from birth until death. At Samhain, the Goddess transforms into her Crone phase and mourns deeply for the God for six weeks until the next Sabbat, Yule. The Goddess entering her Crone phase symbolizes how we must first let go in order for us to be able to move on.

The veil between the worlds of the living and the dead is at it's very thinnest at Samhain. Traditionally, it's the time of year where we try to communicate with those on the other side of the veil, which makes Samhain a powerful time for any form of divination, whether that is tarot, a pendulum, runes or scrying.

Enjoy this transformational period when we hover between the light and the dark, as Samhain marks the midpoint between the Autumn Equinox and the Winter Solstice. Allow yourself to let go of the things that are no longer serving you, and instead look to the new year with optimism.

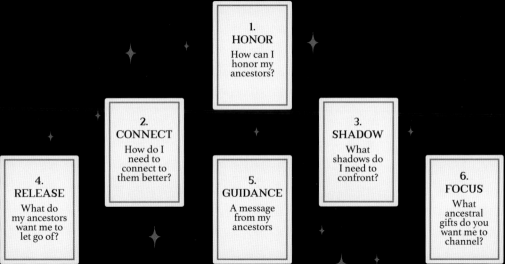

1.
HONOR

How can I honor my ancestors?

2.
CONNECT

How do I need to connect to them better?

3.
SHADOW

What shadows do I need to confront?

4.
RELEASE

What do my ancestors want me to let go of?

5.
GUIDANCE

A message from my ancestors

6.
FOCUS

What ancestral gifts do you want me to channel?

SAMHAIN RITUALS

Create an altar with photos of
ancestors who have passed.

Leave offerings outside for
the dead.

Hold a Dumb Supper for
those who have passed.

Hold a candle ceremony
for your ancestors.

Make a besom to sweep
away negativity.

Cast a family protection
spell and share stories.

Cook family recipes,
using the spices below.

Practice divination.

SAMHAIN CORRESPONDENCES

Cerridwen, Hecate, Lilith,
Osiris, Horned God,
Demeter, Persephone

Citrine, Carnelian,
Ametrine, Moonstone,
Hematite, Botswana, Agate,

Rosemary, Mugwort,
Wormwood, Tarragon, Bay
Leaf, Pine Needles, Nettle

Apples, Nut breads,
Pumpkin, Gingerbread,
Root Vegetables

Sandalwood, Dragon's
Blood, Benzoin,
Patchouli, Cinnamon

SAMHAIN RITUALS
& Spell Correspondence

Samhain rituals don't have to be long or complicated, unless that feels right for you. Sometimes, simple rituals are the most meaningful. There are so many things you can do at Samhain that will help you to connect to nature's seasonal cycle.

A ritual is about performing an established action with intent for a particular purpose. A ritual can be something as simple as lighting a balefire (a Middle-English term for a large outdoor fire); carving a pumpkin, using the action of working with the pumpkin to connect yourself to the grounding and balancing force of nature; or cooking recipes to help you honor those who have passed.

At this time of year, it's common for a practitioner to make an altar upon which they can remember and honor their loved ones who have passed, particularly those who practiced the Craft. If you are the first Witch in your family and don't have blood relatives who followed the Old Ways, you can still honor our brothers and sisters in the Craft who have passed; it's not necessary to be an actual blood relative and it can still can be a very symbolic act.

On your ancestor altar, place items such as photos, personal items owned by the person you want to honor (like a ring), or offerings of their favorite food and drink. Water is also traditionally placed on an altar for any spirits that pass through. If you don't have any photographs, you can write the person's name on a piece of paper and put that on your altar.

If you want to leave an offering for the dead at Samhain, there are lots of options. You could visit a cemetery and place a coin on the grave of a loved one to honor them, or leave an offering of meat, tobacco, dark candles, or coins for the spirits who are traveling through the veil. You can also pour a drink, usually alcohol, into the earth.

Another traditional ritual is holding a Dumb Supper: a meal where you set an extra place at the dinner table and serve an extra plate of food to represent the spirit of the person or people you want to honor. The meal is then eaten in silence, and the food is traditionally thrown away as a mark of respect to the dead.

THE MEANING OF
Yule & Tarot Spread

◇◇◇◇

SYMBOLIZES: Beginnings, cycles, rebirth, rest, gratitude, light and dark

Yule is a Lesser Sabbat that falls between December 21 and 23 in the Northern Hemisphere and June 20 and 23 in the Southern Hemisphere. This astrological event is also known as the Winter Solstice: the time in the year when we have reached the depth of darkness with the coming of the longest night and the shortest day of the year. From this point on, the days get a little longer as we leave the dark half of the year behind. It's a time where the Wheel moves from Waning (decreasing) to Waxing (increasing) with the promise of brighter days to come, and Yule celebrates the eternal cycle of life, death, and rebirth as well as the triumph of the light over the darkness.

Yule is one of the most celebrated of the eight Sabbats as its traditions and customs have become so ingrained in popular culture. Christmas trees, bright lights, gifts, a divine birth, yule logs and many other traditions all have Pagan origins. The lights they light, whether electric or candle, originate from the Pagan tradition of lighting candles and balefires (bonfires) to lure back the Sun and celebrate the coming of lighter, brighter days.

The Winter Solstice is the best day of the year for self-reflection. The longest night of the year provides the darkness we need to look into ourselves. We can evaluate and reflect on the year that has passed, the good and bad things, the things you have learned and the things you want to achieve in the future. It's a time to plant seeds and set goals and intentions for the coming year that will give you opportunities for growth. Yule is a time of quiet energy which makes it the perfect time for rest, recharging our batteries, and self-care.

When the Wheel turns to Yule, the God who died at Samhain is reborn via the Goddess. The Winter Solstice marks the longest day of the year and from this point onward, the days grow longer as we welcome back the Sun. The returning Sun represents the rebirth of the God, sometimes known as the Oak King, who will reign over our longer days and shorter nights. Although his power is still in its infancy, shown by the still relatively short days, the God's power will continue to increase until it reaches its height again at Litha.

YULE

Yule marks the turning of the Wheel from Waning to Waxing, dark to light.

The festival marks the Winter Solstice, the shortest day and the longest night.

It's time to plant seeds, rest, reflect inwardly, and settle in for the colder months.

It marks the beginning of 12 days when we honor the coming of the Sun.

It celebrates the Goddess giving birth to the God known as the Oak King.

It's a fire festival of rebirth and the coming of longer days.

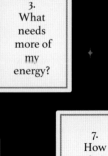

I.
What must I let go?

2.
What seeds do I need to sow?

3.
What needs more of my energy?

4.
What needs less of my energy?

5.
What does the darkness reveal?

6.
What do I need to reflect on?

7.
How do I nourish my soul?

YULE RITUALS &
Spell Correspondence

Yule is probably the easiest Sabbat to celebrate, particularly in the broom closet, because so many of the ancient Yule traditions have found their way into mainstream consciousness. Many are viewed as "traditional" Christmas celebrations so would not raise any suspicions if practiced in the Northern Hemisphere. There are many familiar, yet meaningful rituals such as decorating a Yule tree, making gingerbread, making a Yule log and drinking mulled wine that all have Pagan origins that can be used to celebrate the Sabbat. They can also help you to connect with the season by bringing nature indoors.

Making your own Yule log is a great way to celebrate the Sabbat. The log is decorated with evergreens, candles, pinecones, berries and, traditionally, the gifts people wanted to receive from the Gods. Once you've created your log, there is a simple Yule Log ritual which is a meaningful way of welcoming back the Sun. Bring your Yule log into your home a few weeks before the Winter Solstice to decorate it. On the night of the Solstice, have a fire and burn some of the log, Traditionally, a part of the Yule log is burned every evening until Twelfth Night (the last night of the Twelve Days of Christmas). You can burn herbs like rosemary, cloves, frankincense, and nutmeg on the log, but do not burn mistletoe as it produces toxic smoke.

Evergreens were cut and brought indoors to symbolize rebirth and renewal. They were thought to have power over death because they stayed green all year round. Making an evergreen wreath is a great way to celebrate Yule because evergreens were thought to defeat winter demons, and even hold back the force of death itself.

Another ancient Yule ritual is to make Wassail, an alcoholic drink of hot mulled cider that is used to toast good health. The drink was put in a large cup or chalice (goblet) and was shared among the people present, who would lift the cup before drinking to say "waes hael", to which the response was "drinc hael", meaning "drink and be well". Wassail was thought to drive away evil spirits and ensure a good crop next year, so a glass would then be poured onto the earth to encourage fertility.

A simple recipe for Wassail is 8 cups of apple cider, 2 cups of orange juice, 2 cups of cranberry juice, 2 cups of spiced brandy, 2 cinnamon sticks, 1 tablespoon of cloves, allspice, ginger, and nutmeg to taste (usually 1 tablespoon of each). Place the mixture in a saucepan and simmer on a low heat for two hours.

YULE RITUALS

Make gingerbread.

Watch the Sun rise after the shortest day.

Create an evergreen wreath.

Decorate a Yule log and a Yule tree.

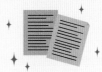

Make time for reflection.

Drink Wassail, mulled wine, or spiced hot chocolate.

Have a balefire (bonfire).

Carve sigils into candles and then light them.

YULE CORRESPONDENCES

Tanzanite, Onyx, Turquoise, Ametrine, Orange, Calcite, Chrysocolla, Garnet

Mistletoe, Holly, Evergreens, Nutmeg, Clove, Cinnamon, Cardamon, Frankincense

Krampus, Holda, Demeter, Ceres, Oak King, Baldur, Dionysus, Frigga, Horus

Cider, Fruit, Nuts, Vegetables, Plum Pudding

Myrrh, Juniper, Cedar, Pine

IMBOLC

Imbolc celebrates the early signs of spring and the passing of winter.

It's a cross-quarter Sabbat, one that is the midpoint between each solstice and equinox.

It's a time where the Goddess Brigid is often honored as the Goddess of the hearth.

The Sun's rebirth is also honored along with the recovery of the Goddesses.

It's a Sabbat of purification, so is a good time to remove things in your life that no longer serve you.

Imbolc is a time to make space for new opportunities and beginnings.

1.
What areas of my life do I need to grow?

2.
How do I nurture this growth?

3.
What should I clear from my life?

4.
How do I facilitate this clearing?

5.
How do I nurture myself?

THE MEANING OF
Imbolc & Tarot Spread

SYMBOLIZES: Rebirth, awakening, cleansing, purifying, seeds, fertility, patience

The Gaelic festival of Imbolc (pronounced "ee-molc") is celebrated from February 1 to Sundown on February 2 in the Northern Hemisphere, and August 1 to 2 in the Southern Hemisphere. The second of the four cross-quarter festivals, and a Greater Sabbat also known as St Brigid's Day, it marks the successful passing of winter and the beginning of a new agricultural cycle. It's the first fire festival and is a celebration of early spring, as the days continue to grow longer, and the first signs of growth begin to shoot up from the cold earth.

This cross-quarter Sabbat (between the Winter Solstice and Spring Equinox) marks the midpoint in winter, and even though the earth might seem mostly dormant and dead, below the ground the energy of the earth is waking up. If we look hard enough, we should be able to see some signs of life in the natural world around us. While Yule was a time to rest and recharge, Imbolc is the time where life begins to stir from its slumbers.

Imbolc celebrates the return of light to the land, and means "in the belly", which refers to the pregnancy of animals like cows and ewes. The days are getting longer, the nights get shorter and the battle between light and dark

favors light once more, helping the seeds in the earth grow. The Goddess, now in her maiden aspect, is recovering from giving birth to the God at Yule, and Brigid, the Irish Goddess of the hearth, fire, childbirth, and midwifery, is honored during Imbolc. She is young and fertile, which is reflected in the fertility of the natural world at this time of year, and her festival was so embedded in Irish culture that the Roman Catholic Church was forced to include Brigid as a saint's day in their calendar and rename it St Brigid's Day.

At Imbolc, the God is still in his child form, but is growing in strength and power, which is where the association with this Sabbat and new opportunities stems from. Like the Goddess who shifts throughout the year between her Maiden/Mother/Crone aspects, the God himself grows and matures from one Sabbat to the next, until he begins to wane and die at Lammas.

Imbolc serves as a reminder to look at the natural world through the eyes of a child to rediscover its beauty and wonder. Celebrating the Sabbats really does help us to form a strong connection with nature and her cycles in a deeper way.

IMBOLC RITUALS

Make a Brigid Cross and
place it on your altar.

Make an Imbolc incense
using the herbs below.

Make a corn dolly.

Spring clean. Use a besom
to sweep away negativity.

Plant seeds in
the ground.

Light a red candle to
honor the Sun.

IMBOLC CORRESPONDENCES

Amethyst, Carnelian,
Calcite, Turquoise, Peridot
Moonstone, Chrysocolla

Cinnamon, Basil,
Rosemary, Wormwood,
Chamomile, Blackberry

Brigid, Danu, Vesta, Diana,
Athena, Gaia

Nuts, Eggs, Dried Fruit,
Dairy products, Lamb,
Seeds

Myrrh, Lavender,
Frankinsense, Jasmine,
Camphor

IMBOLC RITUALS &
Spell Correspondence

Imbolc celebrates the coming of early spring, when nature starts to come alive. Although Yule is concerned with mentally sewing seeds, Imbolc is a time for physically sowing seeds in the soil. The earth may still look and feel asleep, but it's far from dormant! The act of sowing seeds helps to put us in touch with nature and the cycle of life happening all around us. We can appreciate this part of the Wheel of the Year more because it puts us in touch with the growing energy of the earth.

Imbolc is the first of three spring Sabbats, and is associated with cleansing and purifying. You can make a ritual from using a besom or vacuum cleaner to remove any negative or stagnant and unwanted energies from your home. It's not just energies that can be swept away at Imbolc, but it's also a good time to do some physical spring cleaning and decluttering around your home of things you don't use. Use it as an opportunity for clearing everything from your life that no longer serves you on all levels, including people, situations, issues, and material belongings. It will allow you to open yourself up and makes the most of the new opportunities and beginnings associated with Imbolc.

Imbolc is the first of four major fire festivals, so lighting a balefire is one good way to honor the season and welcome the light of the Sun. If you can't have a big fire, light a red candle to symbolize the coming of the lighter days and shorter nights. A good way to start the process of spring cleaning is to write down all the aspects of your life you want to clear away and then burning the list in the fire of the candle. Imbolc isn't just about physical cleaning— it's a good time to clear out mental clutter too.

The Goddess Brigid can be honored in traditional ways such as making a corn dolly, or making a Brigid's Cross. This is an ancient Irish custom where a cross is woven from rushes or straw with a square in the center and the four arms tied at the end. Step-by-step instructions are easily found with a quick internet search. It's sometimes known as a Celtic Sun Wheel, which is a reminder that Imbolc is the festival where the coming of the light from the Sun is celebrated.

THE MEANING OF
Ostara & Tarot Spread

SYMBOLIZES: Fertility, growth, rebirth, new life, purification, balance

Ostara (pronounced "oh-star-ah") is a Lesser Sabbat that falls between March 20 and 23 in the Northern Hemisphere, and September 20 and 23 in the Southern Hemisphere. It is the second spring festival on the Wheel of the Year, and is a celebration of life, growth, fertility, rebirth, and abundance. Ostara is also known as the Spring Equinox, the time when the hours of light and dark are at equal length and in perfect equilibrium. It's a time of balance, not just light and dark but also feminine and masculine, the seen and unseen.

Ostara is named after the Germanic fertility goddess and has been celebrated in different forms for hundreds of years. It's a time when the natural world is flourishing, and the growing fertility of the Goddess can be seen in nature as it begins to burst into bloom. At Ostara, the Goddess is honored in her maiden aspect as she comes into her full power, and the God moves from infancy to greater maturity, reflected in the increasingly lighter days. Ostara is the time of year when the eternal cycle of life, death, and rebirth is complete. Signs of spring can be seen everywhere, and the fertility of the Earth can be both seen and felt.

There's no doubt that the Christian festival of Easter finds many of its roots and spirituality from the Sabbat of Ostara—the names themselves reflect the Pagan influence. Easter is about rebirth, resurrection, and new life, just like Ostara. Another similarity is the role that eggs play in both festivals. The egg is easily one of the most well-known symbols of Ostara. Eggs are a universal sign of new life and they were often carried as fertility amulets and given as gifts.

Ostara is also associated with purification and removing any negative energies. After the Spring Equinox, the time where light and dark are in perfect balance, the Wheel continues to turn and light triumphs over the dark. It's a good time to remove any unwanted or negative energies by continuing the work you began at Imolc by having another mental and physical spring clean. The things that need to be cleared from your life and your space are essential for balance and will create the perfect environment for personal growth and development.

OSTARA

Ostara is the celebration of spring, new life, fertility, and growth.

Ostara is known as the Spring Equinox, when dark and light are equal.

The Goddess is coming into her power and the God is moving toward maturity.

Winter is over but the heat of summer is yet to come, creating a balanced energy.

It's a time of purification, releasing the things that hold us back.

I.
What seeds do I need to plant?

2.
What do I need to cultivate?

3.
What areas of my life need a spring clean?

4.
What parts of my life are out of balance

5.
How can I bring balance to my life?

6.
When I find balance, what will emerge?

OSTARA RITUALS &
Spell Correspondence

Many Ostara traditions will already be very familiar, like the role of the egg in celebrations. Eggs are given to celebrate Easter, the most sacred Christian festival, but the symbol of the egg is Pagan in origin. Painting and giving eggs as gifts is a very easy but meaningful way to celebrate and connect you with the fertility of the natural world.

An egg blessing is a simple ritual to put you in touch with the abundance of Earth. This is where you can say a simple blessing over the egg you've decorated. The blessing can be for abundance, fertility, or growth, and the words can be a simple as "I bless this egg, the symbol of the rebirth of nature and the fertility of the earth. May it bring abundance to my life." Depending on the intentions you have for your workings, afterward you can either eat it if it's a fertility blessing, bury it for workings connected to growth, or use it as a decoration in blessings for abundance.

As the second of three spring festivals, planting seeds is a great way to honor Ostara. Go out into your garden or use a plant pot full of soil and sow some seeds. The act of having physical contact with the earth can have a strong grounding effect that will help you to make the most of the balancing force of the Spring Equinox. You can also practice seed magick where you take some seeds and fill them with a specific intention. Plant them and watch how, as the seeds grow, so does the strength of your intention.

Since Ostara is connected to purification, this is the perfect time to do some spring cleaning. Sweep all the unwanted energies out of you space with a besom or vacuum cleaner and visualize the negative energy leaving as you go. Declutter and tidy up your home and look inward and be honest about the things or people holding you back.

Taking time to get out into nature can really boost the feeling of wellbeing. Go outside and try to look for all the signs of spring in the natural world around you. Stop to notice the buds on the trees, the spring flowers that are in bloom, the shoots emerging from the ground, and listen for any animal noises you can hear. Immerse yourself in the new life shooting forth everywhere as the Earth wakes up.

OSTARA RITUALS

Earth focused meditation.

Purify your home and scatter
eggshells around it for protection.

Go for a walk to look for
signs of spring.

Decorate your home
with spring flowers.

Set up an altar with flowers,
eggs, and rabbits.

Decorate eggs and give
them as gifts.

Plant seeds for purifying
plants such as rosemary.

OSTARA CORRESPONDENCES

Amethyst, Bloodstone,
Canelian, Onyx, Lapis,
Lazuli, Jade, Kynite

Violet, Tulip, Daffodil, Rose,
Jasmine, Iris, Cinquefoil,
Honeysuckle, Narcissus

Cernunnos, Odin, Athena,
Gaia, Osiris, Aphrodite

Cheese, Eggs, Seeds, Nuts,
Seasonal Vegetables, Honey

African Violet, Jasmine,
Rose, Frankincense,
Sandalwood

BELTANE

Beltane celebrates the start of summer. It's a fire festival that celebrates new life.

Beltane celebrates the sexual union between the God and Goddess.

It's a joyful celebration with fire jumping and dancing around the May Pole.

The Goddess is pregnant and her fertility can be seen in nature.

The earth's energies are strong and life is bursting with abundance.

1.
What do
I need to
leave in
the past?

2.
What am
I ready
to bring
forth in
my life?

5.
How do I
facilitate
this
growth?

3.
What part
of my life
must be
reborn?

4.
How can I
manifest
abundance?

THE MEANING OF
Beltane & Tarot Spread

◇◇◇◇

SYMBOLIZES: Fertility, new life, creation, growth, abundance, passion, union

Beltane (pronounced "Bell-tayne" or "Beel-teen") is a Greater Sabbat that falls on May 1 in the Northern Hemisphere and October 31 in the Southern Hemisphere. The third cross-quarter festival of the year, it marks the peak of spring and the beginnings of summer, and is the Gaelic May Day Sabbat of fire, creation, and sexuality, as the fertility returns to the Earth. In the Southern Hemisphere, Beltane falls on Novey Eve.

This Sabbat, which falls midway between the Spring Equinox and the Summer Solstice, is the third and final springtime festival, and the third fire festival on the Wheel of the Year. Life itself is celebrated at the time when the Earth's energies are at their strongest, and creation is bursting with abundant potency.

At Beltane, everything in the natural world is at the peak of its fertility, and this is the time when potential has finally transformed into actual conception. Nature is literally bursting with energy—blossoms are on the trees, flowers are in bloom, and buds are unfurling. This is truly a joyous celebration full of music, song, sensuality, light, and merriment at the coming of the light half of the year.

Beltane celebrates the divine feminine. In the Northern Hemisphere, the Goddess manifests as the May Queen, while the God emerges as the May King or Jack in the Green. At this point in the year, the God and Goddess are youthful and strong. In both hemispheres, Beltane celebrates them finally coming together in sexual union to create new life. Their union not only ensures the fertility of the Earth as the Goddess becomes pregnant (she will eventually give birth to the God at Yule) but also the coming of light, after the dark depths of winter. Now we honor the Goddess as she steps into her Mother aspect, and the never-ending cycle of life, death, and rebirth continues.

The world "Beltane" originates from the Celtic word meaning "Bright Fire", which shows how central fire is to the festivities on this Sabbat. It represents the light half of the year as well as the passion and vitality of the union between the God and the Goddess. Beltane is about creation and you can channel this creative energy in all aspects of your life if you reach out to connect to the creation within nature.

BELTANE RITUALS

Decorate with flowers, wreaths and garlands.

Make a flower crown with the flowers below.

Wash your face with the dew of dawn.

Light a balefire (bonfire).

Create a ritual to honor the Sacred Feminine.

Fertility magick.

BELTANE CORRESPONDENCES

Malachite, Tiger's Eye, Carnelian, Bloodstone, Rose Quartz, Emerald

Woodruff, Mugwort, Cowslip, Dandelions, Tulips, Rowan

Horned God, Diana, Fraya, Odin, Pan, Flora

Honey, Dairy, Fresh Vegetables, Light Cakes

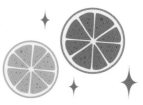

Frankincense, Citrus, Jasmine, Ylang-Ylang, Pine, Mint

BELTANE RITUALS &
Spell Correspondence

Many of the rituals and activities associated with Beltane are related to the themes of new life, creation, and fertility, all of which help us to connect to the powerful and potent energy of the Earth.

At Beltane, flowers like lily of the valley, lilacs, and freesias are all in bloom and play a big part in May Day celebrations. Bring the outside, inside, and decorate your home or space with spring flowers to symbolize the fertility of nature. I recommend including budding hawthorn branches in your decorations as they're traditionally brought inside as a symbol of abundance and new life. Rowan twigs can also be used for decoration by hanging them above your hearth (if you have one) as a home blessing. Wreaths and garlands can be made from greenwood and brought in to attract abundance.

Making flower crowns at Beltane is another traditional ritual to represent the crown of the May Queen in all her fertility. It's a simple way of welcoming nature's abundance into your own life and helping you to connect with natural world. Another way to truly connect with the natural world is by washing your face with the dew of the May Day dawn as it was thought to bring good health, luck, and beauty.

As Beltane is a fire festival, the Sabbat is traditionally celebrated by lighting a balefire. If you are able to have a fire, it can be as big or small as you want. You could even light a small fire in your cauldron or in a fireproof dish with some paper and lemon peel. An old tradition is to jump over the fire to cleanse, purify, and bring fertility.

Fertility symbols, as well as flowers, are good items for decorating your altar. If, like me, space is an issue for you, your altar doesn't need to be elaborate. It could be as simple as a vase of spring flowers to represent the fertility of the Earth and a brown, green, or white candle for abundance.

Beltane is a time for love and passion, which is why it is the perfect time for Handfastings. This Pagan wedding ceremony might not be an option, but if not, this is still a time when couples can recommit to one another and to their relationship in the spirit of the Sabbat.

THE MEANING OF
Litha & Tarot Spread

◇◇◇◇

SYMBOLIZES: Power, warmth, abundance, divination, fire, growth, love

Litha, known as Summer Solstice and Midsummer, is a Lesser Sabbat that falls between June 20 and 23 in the Northern Hemisphere and December 20 and 23 in the Southern Hemisphere. It celebrates the longest day of the year and the shortest night as the Sun is at the height of its power. From this point on, the Sun's energy will wane, days will get shorter, and the Wheel will turn to the dark half of the year.

Litha is a Sabbat of contrasts. Though it marks the longest day, it signals that the days to follow will begin to get shorter and darker as the Sun begins to wane and the Wheel keeps moving. The awareness of what is to come helps us see and have a greater appreciation for the changing of the seasons, which can have a strong and grounding affect upon us.

The light and warm summer days are Waning and the coming of the harvest is celebrated. At Litha, the Goddess is pregnant from her union with the God at Beltane, and shifts to her mother aspect. She takes on the archetype of Mother Earth and is blooming. The Sun God (or Oak King), who prepares to decline over the dark half of the year, reaches the height of his potency on this, the longest day of the year.

While the God is powerful now, the days begin to shorten from this point as he prepares to die. His powers as the Sun God will begin to wane as the strength of the Holly King, who rules over the dark half of the year, increases. This rising of one king causes the death of the other, and serves as a further reminder that the Wheel never stops turning, and the cycle of birth, death, and rebirth is never-ending.

In connection with the agricultural calendar, Litha celebrates abundance as crops have reached their full maturity, and the first of the three harvests begin. It's a time to celebrate the growth of the seeds that were planted in the in the spring. It's also time to celebrate the manifestation of any metaphorical seeds you planted at this time that have since come into being.

Litha, also known as the Summer Solstice, celebrates the longest day of the year.

This Lesser Sabbat celebrates crops reaching their full maturity.

It is a Sabbat of contrast as the dark half of the year begins to loom.

The Goddess is pregnant and flourishing. The God is at the height of his power.

The Oak King weakens as the Holly King strengthens.

It's a time to celebrate the growth of the seeds planted in early spring.

I.
What must I release from the shadows

2.
What must I do to release them?

3.
Where are my opportunities for growth?

4.
What should I focus my attention on to aid growth?

5.
Advice for the dark half of the year.

LITHA RITUALS &
Spell Correspondence

There is a vast array of small, meaningful rituals that can be performed to celebrate the Summer Solstice. During this Sabbat, like many others, lighting a fire is at the center of the celebrations, and represents the Sun at the peak of its power. This fire can be as large or small as you want and you can burn herbs such as yarrow, rose, lavender, and mugwort. After the fire has been left to go out, it's traditional for the cold ashes to be put on the crops to ensure a good harvest. Save your own fire ash for any plants you have (inside and out) or for use in any abundance and fertility magick.

This time of year is a traditional time for herb picking, particularly herbs intended for magick and medicines. Go out into nature to forage for different herbs to use in your workings. A beautiful incense blend for the Summer Solstice is 1 part thyme, 1 part rosemary, 1 part lavender, 1 part chamomile and ½ part rose.

At Litha, the simple act of watching the Sun rise on the morning of the Solstice is a beautiful, simple ritual that doesn't involve any special tools or ingredients, and is a reminder of the Sun's power and warmth. Another simple ritual is to place a jar or bowl of water in the sunlight an hour before midday and leave it to charge for a few hours. Sun water is bursting with energy and is good for removing strong negative and unwanted energies. It also gives a powerful boost to your magick and can be used in rituals as an offering to any Sun deity.

At the time when Earth is at the peak of its energy, use this time to ground yourself. Grounding is like meditation, but it allows us to live in the present, re-center ourselves and reconnect to the earth. There are many grounding techniques, including walking barefoot on the ground to allow the earth's energy to flow into your body. A technique I've used for years when I feel disconnected is to look around and name five things you can see, four things you can hear, three things you can touch, two things you can smell and one thing you can taste. It's a good way of bringing you back to the present moment by connecting you to the world around you, and doing this exercise when you are among nature will boost its grounding effect.

LITHA RITUALS

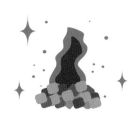

Perform a fire ritual and connect to the element.

Light a red/yellow candle to celebrate the Sun.

Forage for herbs for magick and medicine.

Go on a nature walk and look for faeries.

Make Sun water.

Wear yellow, orange, red, and gold.

Watch the sunrise.

LITHA CORRESPONDENCES

Carnelian, Citrine, Sunstone, Tigers Eye, Peridot, Amber, Rose Quartz

Honeysuckle, Daisy, Mugwort, Vervain, Rosemary, Fern, Yarrow

Aphrodite, Athena, Brigid, Cerridwen, Thor, Odin, Lugh

Citrus fruit, Dairy, Honey, Pine Nuts, Grapes, Seeds

Sandalwood, Rose, Lavender, Citrus, Pine

LAMMAS

The last fire festival, it marks the end of the summer and the start of fall.

It's time to give thanks for the abundance of the harvest.

It's the celebration of the first harvest.

The Wheel turns and we move into the dark half of the year.

The God Lugh sacrifices himself for the sake of the harvest.

I.
What seeds have I been sowing lately?

2.
Which seeds need more time to mature?

3.
What seeds are ready to harvest?

4.
What is abundant in my life?

THE MEANING OF
Lammas & Tarot Spread

◇◇◇◇

SYMBOLIZES: First harvest, celebration, reflection, gratitude, sacrifice

Lammas (also known as Lughnasadh or Lughnasa) is a Greater Sabbat that falls on August 1 in the Northern Hemisphere and February 1 in the Southern Hemisphere. It is the final of the four cross-quarter festivals, and is also known "Lammas" (pronounced "Lam-mas"), a Celtic name given to this Sabbat in remembrance of Lugh, the God of light (or the Sun God).

At Lammas, Lugh dies when the grain is harvested. Lugh's sacrifice is honored as he shifts his energy into the first grain to ensure a good crop. The power of the Sun ripens the grain, and the seeds are saved for next year's crop, when the Waning Sun God will have enough energy to ripen them in spring.

Lammas is the first of three harvests and the last fire festival of the year. From this point onward, the days continue to shorten until the Autumn Equinox. The word "Lammas" is derived from the Anglo-Saxon word meaning "loaf", and bread is central to this harvest festival. Grain was so important to many ancient civilizations, as it was thought to be a symbol of the cycle of life, death, and rebirth.

Lammas is a celebration of the bounty the Earth has given, and a reminder that there are still two harvests left and a great deal of hard work to do. This celebration gives us the opportunity to reflect and be grateful for the bounty we have in our own lives, but also to remember that we must not lose sight of the larger picture. We are in the dark half of the year, and even though the Sun is still shining and warming the Earth, fall (autumn) has started, and summer is now over. The cycle is Waning again, even though it will take months before the leaves on the trees begin to change.

It's not just Lugh who is remembered at Lammas. The Goddess is celebrated in her mother aspect and is known as the Grain Mother, Harvest Mother, Earth Mother, and Harvest Queen. For the last time, the God and Goddess lie with each other before the God dies. The Goddess is heavily pregnant, and her radiance is reflected in the natural world, which helps us to appreciate that this is just one part on a neverending cycle. The Goddess then moves slowly toward her Crone phase as the Wheel turns closer to Yule. Like every Sabbat on the Wheel, you do not have to honor any Gods and Goddesses if that direction feels wrong or doesn't resonate with the path you are walking. It is purely a personal choice and you can still celebrate the Sabbats simply by celebrating and connecting with the changes of the seasons around you.

LAMMAS RITUALS

Make corn dollies.

Decorate an altar with grains, nuts, and yellow candles.

Practice gratitude.

Make bread or an apple pie, carving sigils onto the top.

Forage for herbs for future spells.

Save seeds to plant next year.

LAMMAS CORRESPONDENCES

Aventurine, Citrine, Topaz, Obsidian, Moss, Clear Quartz, Carnelian, Onyx

Basil, Rosemary, Cornstalks, Frankinsense, Heather, Myrtle, Sunflower, Wheat

Dana, Diana, Hecate, Apollo, Osari, Demeter, Isis

Apples, Wheat, Corn, Barley, Nuts, Carrots

Frankincense, Ecualyptus, Passionflower, Sandalwood

LAMMAS RITUALS &
Spell Correspondence

Lammas is a time to give thanks for the first harvest, while keeping an eye on the future and all that must to be done in the remaining two harvests. As the Wheel keeps turning and we move further into the dark half of the year, make some space for reflection. Think about the seeds you planted in the spring and if some of them have already manifested. If they have, they are your first harvest. If there are some that have yet to mature and grow, it's a good time to reflect about how you can help them mature and bear fruit. Make sure your intentions are focused and well defined and that you are doing everything, both physically and mentally, to manifest your goals.

It's also a time to practice gratitude. Just as the Celts celebrated the first harvest, give thanks for the seeds that have matured and for the good things in your life. These are metaphorical seeds, but it's also good to save actual seeds from flowers and crops to plant and grow next spring.

As this Sabbat celebrates grain, making bread is a perfect activity as it can help you appreciate how much energy it takes to make and to reflect therefore on how precious it was to our ancestors. It's a traditional way to connect with the changing of the seasons and where we are on the cycle. Bringing in seasonal flowers such as sunflowers, lilies, and lavender into your home or space is another good way to honor Lammas in a low-key manner.

Making corn dollies, usually from a dried corn husk, is another very traditional way to celebrate Lammas since it was understood that the spirit of the corn moved into the husks after harvest.

Getting outside might not sound like a ritual in itself, but going out into nature around the time of the Sabbats truly helps you to reconnect with the cycles and the natural world. It's easy today to fall out of touch with nature because our busy lives can leave us very little free time, but our connection to nature helps to nourish and balance us, so if your connection has weakened, it can have a negative impact on your wellbeing. Get out into nature and look intently at the life around you. Feel the warmth of the Sun and reconnect to the everlasting cycle of life, death, and rebirth happening all around you.

THE MEANING OF
Mabon & Tarot Spread

SYMBOLIZES: Balance, gratitude, death, dark and light, preparation

Mabon (pronounced "May-bon") falls between September 20 and 23 in the Northern Hemisphere and March 20 and 23 in the Southern Hemisphere. It's also known as the Autumn Equinox. It's the time where the length of day and night are equal and in perfect balance, and we celebrate the triumph of the darkness over the light. Mabon is also the second harvest of the cycle, a time when the grain has been brought in, and only winter plants remain in the ground.

It is around now that we start to feel that fall (autumn) is finally upon us, as the leaves start to turn gold, red, and brown and all the fields are nearly empty. The cycle is still Waning and there's a sense of winding down in the natural world. Harvest time is the busiest time in the agricultural year, so Mabon gives us the opportunity to relax, enjoy ourselves, and be thankful for the fruits of our labors. It's also a reminder for us to try and work to gain more balance in our own lives, particularly our work/rest balance.

At Mabon, the God finally dies, and begins his journey to the Underworld after sacrificing himself for the sake of the first harvest at Lammas. The God retreats from the world and as he departs, he takes the warmth and power of the Sun with him, which turns the weather colder. The Goddess, now in her Crone phase, is growing old, even though she is still pregnant, but she misses the God so much that she decides to follow him to the Underworld. As she departs, she also withdraws her power and energy, which makes the leaves on the trees die off.

There is no historical evidence that this Sabbat was called anything but the Autumn Equinox until the 1970s when Aidan Kelly, the founder of the Covenant of the Goddess, began to use Mabon as a name. Since then, this has become a popular name for the Sabbat. Interestingly, the word Mabon does appear in historical documents, but as a name and not a festival. The name came from the Welsh God "Mabon ap Madron", meaning "The Son of the Mother". Welsh stories speak of a divine birth, and a boy from a divine mother. Sound familiar? We can identify this theme with the pregnant Goddess carrying the God to be born at Yule.

MABON

Mabon celebrates the second harvest. The day and night are now equal length.

Rest as nature starts winding down and the cycle continues to wane.

It's a time to reflect on the blessings in our lives.

The Autumn Equinox is a reminder to strive for balance in our own lives.

The Goddess follows the God to the Underworld, causing leaves to die.

It's a time to celebrate the growth of the seeds planted in early spring.

I.
What needs to be harvested in my life?

2.
How do I welcome balance into my life?

3.
What areas of my life need balance?

4.
What good will emerge from the darkness?

5.
How can I continue to grow?

MABON RITUALS &
Spell Correspondence

Apple magick is practiced at Mabon and can be as simple as peeling an apple (the color doesn't matter) and burying the peel in the ground to symbolize the birth, death, and rebirth cycle. Eat the peeled apple to take in its wisdom and lessons you need to learn. You can then save the apple seeds for use in magick related to love, fertility, wisdom, beauty, and fidelity.

Apples represent the second harvest, and many traditions consider them to be symbols of wholeness, wisdom, and guidance. They are also associated with the Goddess as the seeds form a star, much like a pentagram when cut vertically. Apples can be used in many rituals and activities to celebrate Mabon. Apple picking is a popular activity, as is getting creative in the kitchen and making apple pie or crumbles and cobblers.

Mabon is the time we give thanks for all that Mother Nature has given us, and is a great time practice gratitude for the blessings in our lives. One of my favorite ways to practice gratitude is to make your own incense. As you grind and mix the herbs and resins, fill them with thanks for the blessings in your life. When you burn it, the smoke will carry your gratitude up into the universe. This incense recipe is perfect for the Mabon: 1 part pine, 1 part juniper, 1 part frankincense, 1 part sandalwood, and 1 part rosemary.

During Mabon, continue the ritual of going outside into nature on each of the Sabbats as a way to connect with the cycles of the seasons. Collect fall (autumn) finds like leaves and conkers to decorate your home, space, or altar, and take time to look at the leaves on the trees in all their fall (autumnal) beauty. Hearing the rustle of leaves on the ground, and completely immersing yourself in the seasonal changes you can see all around can have a stabilizing and grounding effect.

The Autumn Equinox is a reminder that we often need to bring more balance into our lives. It is an opportunity to reflect on your life and ask yourself what areas of your life are currently out of balance. Light a black and a white candle to represent this balance as you reflect on practical thoughts of how you can help to bring about the change that will enable you to reach an equilibrium.

MABON RITUALS

Create a spell or ritual using
the correspondences below.

Practice apple magick.

Go on a nature walk and
pick apples.

Decorate an altar with candles
and fruits of the harvest.

Make incense using
the herbs below.

MABON CORRESPONDENCES

Hematite, Amber, Citrine,
Ametrine, Rhodonite,
Topaz, Lapis Lazuli

Bay Leaves, Yarrow, Hyssop,
Rue, Rosemary, Chamomile,
Rosehips, Juniper, Pine

Mabon, Thor, Persephone,
The Green Man, Demeter,
Minerva

Apples, Wheat, Carrots,
Corn, Melons

Cinnamon, Cedar,
Frankincense, Myrrh,
Pine, Sandalwood

FULL MOON

WAXING
GIBBOUS

WANING
GIBBOUS

FIRST
QUARTER

THIRD
QUARTER

GROW &
LET GO

WAXING
CRESCENT

WANING
CRESCENT

NEW MOON

3

THE MOON

We are far more connected to the cycles of the Moon than most people appreciate. In our busy lives, it's easy to get out of sync with the natural world. The Moon has long been associated with magick and Witchcraft, and each phase is associated with a different kind of energy. If we can learn to connect with the energies of the Moon during all her phases, she can teach us how to wait, how to grow, but also how to let go. She can teach us so much about ourselves if we are willing to listen, and aligning with her phases can help life run more smoothly and feel more balanced, which can have a positive impact on our sense of wellbeing.

Timing your spells to the phases of the Moon is a great way to add power and energy to your workings. In this chapter, we'll look at the eight Moon phases in detail, the different kinds of magick associated with them, and the rituals you can perform to help you connect with the power of the Moon. These rituals don't need to be elaborate, but they can help you to achieve your goals.

NEW MOON
Day 1

The New Moon is the first phase of the lunar cycle. The Moon is not visible in the sky at this time as the Sun is behind it, so illuminates the surface facing away from Earth. The New Moon is associated with fresh starts, so is a good time to begin new and creative projects. It's the point in the lunar cycle where you take the initial steps toward manifesting your goals, so its also the perfect time for reflection and for setting new intentions. It's a time to plan how you will work toward your goals and the steps you need to take to support your intentions. Journaling is a good ritual for the New Moon and can help the planning and reflective process.

The association with new starts makes this Moon cycle a perfect time for cleansing. Use this opportunity to cleanse yourself by taking a ritual salt bath and cleaning your home or altar space. I like to burn rosemary, juniper, and lavender but there are other methods and herbs for cleansing (see page 32) to start the new lunar cycle with a clean slate. The New Moon is also associated with banishing and deconstructive magick, which is the magickal act of removing unwanted energy from your life. It is seen by some as manipulative magick as it impacts on the free will of others, while other practitioners are comfortable to use this kind of magick. It is a personal choice that should be made based on your own feelings. If banishing is something you are comfortable with, the New Moon provides the perfect time to remove people, mental baggage, negative thinking, or indeed anything that no longer serves your life in the present and stands in the way of your growth.

The New Moon can make some people feel more anxious, agitated, and tired, which is nature's way of syncing us with the rhythms of the Moon as an act of self-care. This is the part of the cycle for some down time where you can make some space to recharge your batteries. Rest is a ritual and it is often the one most needed but overlooked. If you are feeling drained around this time, don't push yourself to do any workings that will deplete your personal energy further. You can't pour from an empty cup. First, you must take care of yourself.

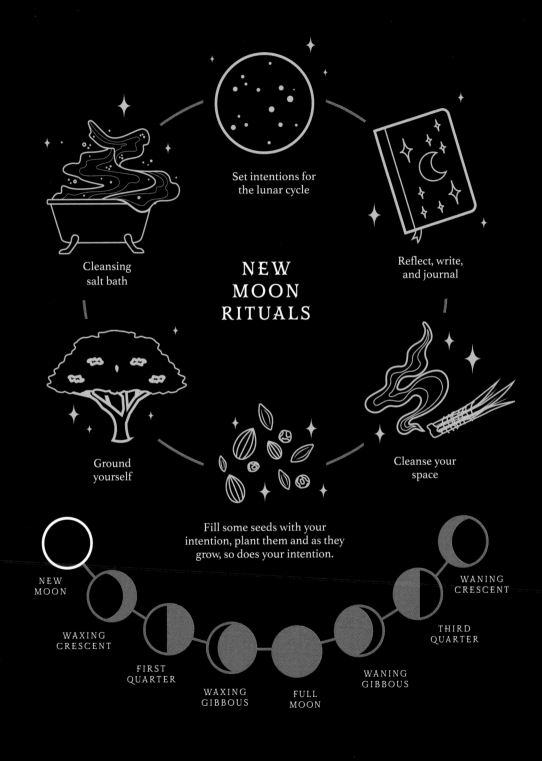

Set intentions for
the lunar cycle

Cleansing
salt bath

Reflect, write,
and journal

NEW MOON RITUALS

Ground
yourself

Cleanse your
space

Fill some seeds with your
intention, plant them and as they
grow, so does your intention.

NEW
MOON

WANING
CRESCENT

WAXING
CRESCENT

THIRD
QUARTER

FIRST
QUARTER

WANING
GIBBOUS

WAXING
GIBBOUS

FULL
MOON

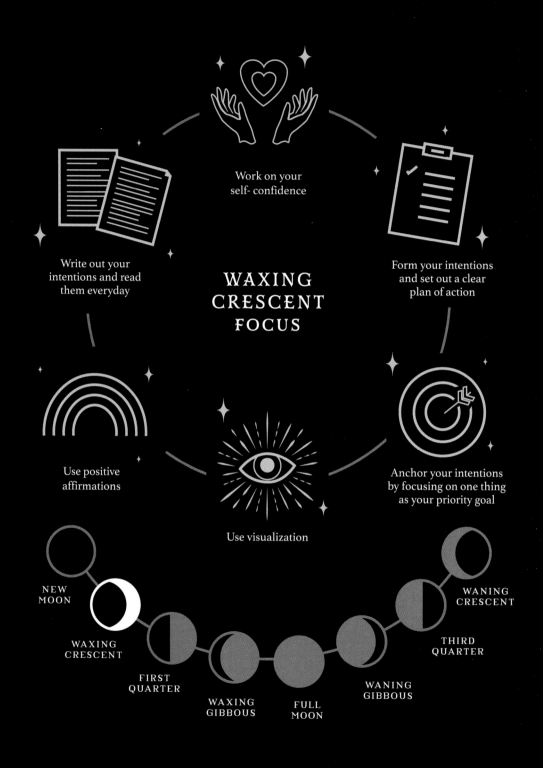

Work on your
self- confidence

Form your intentions
and set out a clear
plan of action

Write out your
intentions and read
them everyday

WAXING
CRESCENT
FOCUS

Anchor your intentions
by focusing on one thing
as your priority goal

Use positive
affirmations

Use visualization

NEW
MOON

WANING
CRESCENT

WAXING
CRESCENT

THIRD
QUARTER

FIRST
QUARTER

WAXING
GIBBOUS

FULL
MOON

WANING
GIBBOUS

WAXING CRESCENT
Day 3

As the Sun starts to move closer to the Moon, it begins to illuminate the right-hand side of the lunar surface to make a crescent shape in the sky. The energies of the Moon are starting to grow and are highly magnetic, making it a great time for constructive magick and for workings that pull things toward you such as prosperity, a new job, and abundance. It's time to refine and organize the intentions you made at the New Moon, so you can anchor them and do all that's necessary to manifest and actualize them.

The Waxing Crescent Moon is a reminder that without good, clear plans, our intentions will never be more than that—just good intentions. Although intentions are powerful, intentions alone will not help you manifest the things you want; you must also do all you can physically and mentally to achieve them. You must be ready to do the mundane work to actualize them. This could mean something like changing your negative mindset or any negative behaviors that inhibit your ability to accomplish your intentions. This Moon phase provides the energy you need to make the necessary changes so you can slowly draw all you want toward you. It helps you to pull all your plans together, so you have a clear strategy of what you want to do next.

As the Moon slowly builds up its power and energy, it's a good time for workings that build up self-confidence and self-worth so you can work on trusting and believing in yourself more. As this time in the lunar cycle encourages you to bring what you want into your life, visualization is a powerful tool to help the process. Don't be tempted to try and visualize more than one thing at once but keep it simple so you don't dilute the power of your energy. Visualize the thing you want in as much detail as possible, imagine how it would feel to attain it and how it would change your life in a positive way. Visualize and affirm it every day alongside your clear plans to harness the Waxing Moon's energy to drive you and your intentions forward. This Moon phase is also associated with positive magick and workings that can help you find your focus if you are struggling to find yours. It's a time to be positive, motivated, and ready to back up your intentions with action. The Moon will provide you with the energy you need to help reel in your intentions.

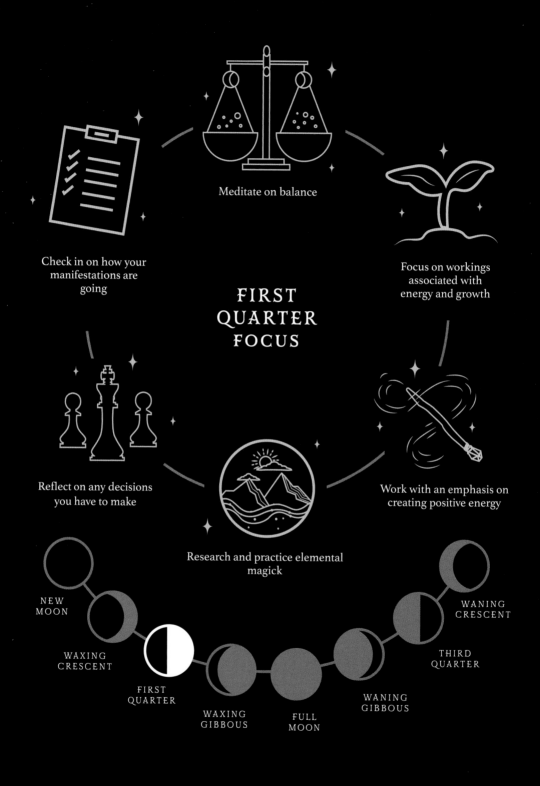

Meditate on balance

Check in on how your
manifestations are
going

Focus on workings
associated with
energy and growth

FIRST
QUARTER
FOCUS

Reflect on any decisions
you have to make

Work with an emphasis on
creating positive energy

Research and practice elemental
magick

NEW
MOON

WAXING
CRESCENT

FIRST
QUARTER

WAXING
GIBBOUS

FULL
MOON

WANING
GIBBOUS

THIRD
QUARTER

WANING
CRESCENT

FIRST QUARTER
Day 7

At this point in the lunar cycle, the whole right-hand side of the Moon is illuminated. It doesn't look like a quarter Moon at all and is sometimes known as "the half-Moon". In this phase, the light and the darkness of the Moon are equal, which can help to show how important balance is to our sense of wellbeing. Every part of the lunar cycle marks a different phase of the journey of your intentions from conception to manifestation, and the First Quarter is no different. At the New Moon, intentions were made, at the Waxing Crescent Moon these intentions were refined. Now, at the First Quarter, it's time to take action and start focusing on working toward your goals. There is more energy available at this point in the cycle, so this can offer an energetic boost to help manifest your intentions. This boost can help to bring a sense of excitement and enthusiasm that will help you to keep moving forward. This makes the First Quarter an excellent time for workings associated with strength and the growth of inner energies and in relationships.

With this extra energetic boost, it can also help you to make difficult decisions, especially if you've been struggling to do so recently. This initial energy is also helpful if you run into any issues, need to break through old patterns of behavior, or find any obstacles standing in your way, as it gives you the energy you need to overcome them and keep the momentum going. The First Quarter symbolizes a period of determination and commitment to action, so although you might run into problems along the way, feel encouraged by the knowledge that they will not hold you back as long as you keep your eyes focused on the intentions you want to bring into being.

The First Quarter is also associated with pausing for a time. If you face some issues or things aren't running as smoothly as they could be, use this time to reflect on where you are in terms of your intentions. Keep your mind clearly focused on what you want to manifest but take some time to re-evaluate your plans in the light of any issues you come up against. This phase is about being receptive to any changes you need to make so you can refocus your energy on what you want to bring into being.

WAXING GIBBOUS
Day 11

At this point in the lunar cycle, more than half the Moon is illuminated, and only a small sliver of dark is left. Now is the time to focus on your intentions as you enter the final stages of planning. The Moon is still in its constructive phase, which means you have time to really hone your plans and goals. Focus really is the key word for this phase in the lunar cycle, and it's time to look at your goals to refine them one last time before the Full Moon, the time of manifestation. Review them honestly and be ready to assess which are realistic and achievable, as this isn't the time for chasing impossible dreams that won't grow and bear fruit. If some goals are unachievable, don't waste your energy but instead redirect your attentions to the realistic ones that just need that extra little push to reach them. The Waxing Gibbous Moon provides the momentum needed for you to accomplish these goals.

There is a good chance that the goals you've been working toward during this lunar cycle are starting to feel like they are aligning. The extra energy on offer from the Waxing Gibbous Moon provides more momentum to help you across the finish line. This is why this Moon phase is particularly associated with spells connected with success in all kinds of projects and areas of life. The time of manifestation and the peak of the Moon's energy is only a few days away and this is your last chance to focus on the expansion and growth of your plans. It's a reminder that the manifestation process doesn't give instant results, and often we must wait for our intentions and goals to come to full maturity in their own time. This makes this Moon phase the perfect time for any workings associated with increase, growth, and drawing things toward you.

Each part of the lunar cycle can have a different effect on us all, and sometimes the Waxing Gibbous Moon, rather than giving us a boost of energy, can make us feel like our plans are on hold. It's not necessarily because your plans are unachievable, but rather your plans are still growing and there is a great deal of change happening beneath the surface. When a seed is planted, it grows significantly in the soil before a shoot is seen above the ground; this can be the same for the Waxing Gibbous Moon.

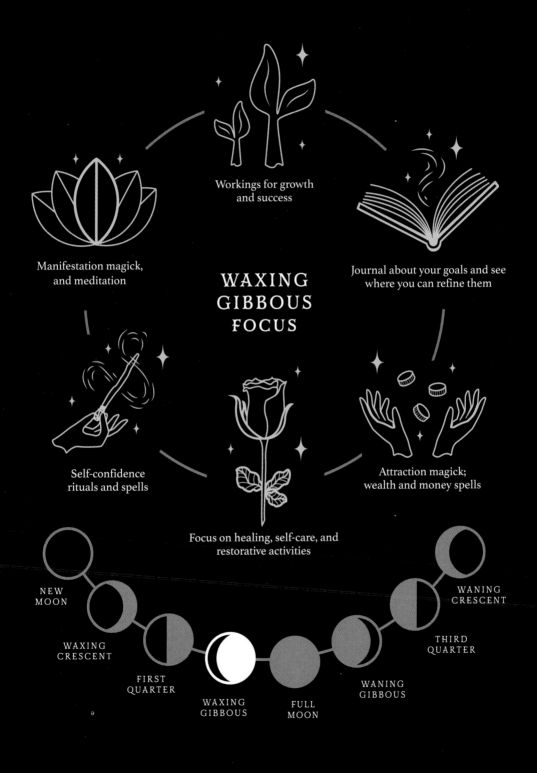

Workings for growth
and success

Manifestation magick,
and meditation

Journal about your goals and see
where you can refine them

WAXING
GIBBOUS
FOCUS

Self-confidence
rituals and spells

Attraction magick;
wealth and money spells

Focus on healing, self-care, and
restorative activities

NEW
MOON

WAXING
CRESCENT

WANING
CRESCENT

THIRD
QUARTER

WAXING
CRESCENT

FIRST
QUARTER

WAXING
GIBBOUS

FULL
MOON

WANING
GIBBOUS

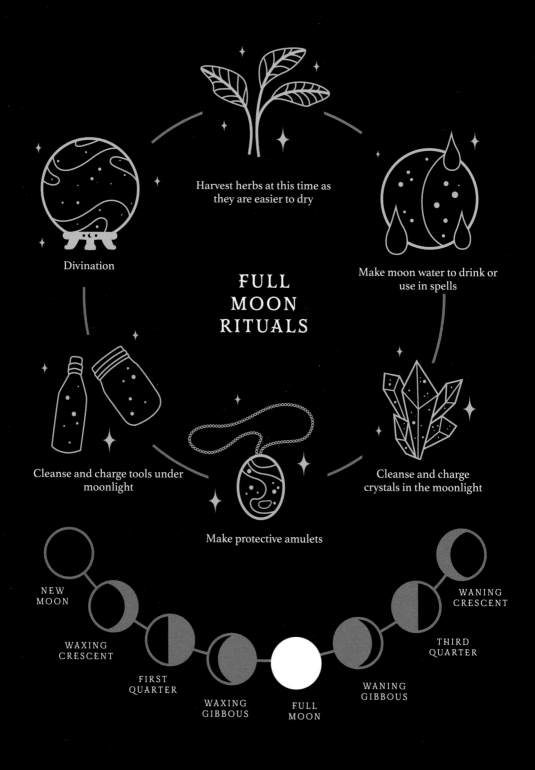

Harvest herbs at this time as they are easier to dry

Divination

FULL
MOON
RITUALS

Make moon water to drink or use in spells

Cleanse and charge tools under moonlight

Cleanse and charge crystals in the moonlight

Make protective amulets

NEW
MOON

WAXING
CRESCENT

FIRST
QUARTER

WAXING
GIBBOUS

FULL
MOON

WANING
GIBBOUS

THIRD
QUARTER

WANING
CRESCENT

FULL MOON
Days 13–15

The Full Moon is the most celebrated of all the Moon phases in the lunar cycle due to its association with power. The Moon is fully illuminated, and at the peak of its energy, so provides the power we need to overcome any challenges we may face and gives an energetic boost to our intentions. This is the time to manifest the goals you've been working toward as things begin to come to fruition. The seeds of intention that were planted at the New Moon are now in full bloom, which represents transformation, abundance, fertility, and completion. Now is the time to manifest your goals and harvest the results.

The Full Moon is a time for protection, healing, and guidance. It's a good time to for tarot/oracle readings, scrying, and any other forms of divination (see Chapter 8). You could even charge your divination tools in the moonlight before you work with them, charge and cleanse crystals and jewelry, as well as making moon water. Take make moon water, place a covered jar/bottle full of water (from the tap is fine!) in the moonlight for at least two hours to charge and bring it inside before the Sun rises. It can then be used to add power to workings, for protection, to water plants, and it can even be consumed to give you an extra boost of energy.

The Full Moon may be a time for intuition and creativity, but also for workings associated with banishing and letting go. Once the Moon reaches the peak of the energy, it slowly begins to wane. It's the opportunity to release everything that inhibits your personal growth. This could be thoughts, people, or emotions—anything that doesn't support or align with your higher self and purpose. This release of lunar energy provides the energetic boost needed for spells and rituals and any other workings that require a decrease of energy.

The Full Moon can often make us feel energized, but it's also common for the energies to be very intense and emotionally draining. If you are low on personal energy, or you feel tired, ill, in pain, or just not in the right headspace, consider postponing your workings until your energy is restored and balanced. Your workings could be less successful if the energy you bring is low or off balance. Use this phase to listen to your body, nourish yourself, and recharge your batteries.

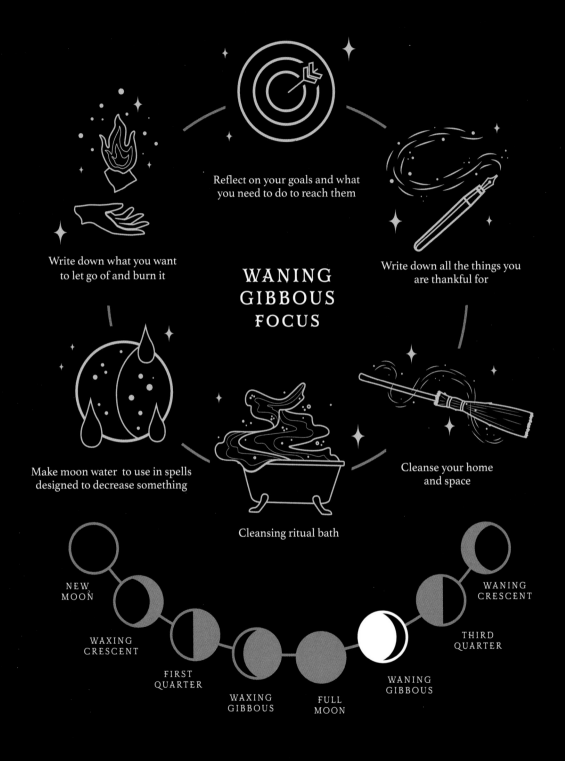

Reflect on your goals and what
you need to do to reach them

Write down what you want
to let go of and burn it

Write down all the things you
are thankful for

WANING
GIBBOUS
FOCUS

Make moon water to use in spells
designed to decrease something

Cleanse your home
and space

Cleansing ritual bath

NEW
MOON

WAXING
CRESCENT

FIRST
QUARTER

WAXING
GIBBOUS

FULL
MOON

WANING
GIBBOUS

THIRD
QUARTER

WANING
CRESCENT

WANING GIBBOUS MOON
Day 18

After the Moon has reached the peak of its power, its size and energy begin to wane as the Sun moves away, creating a shadow on the right-hand side of the lunar surface. The Moon will continue to wane until the New Moon when the cycle begins all over again. After the time of high and often overwhelming power of the Full Moon, the waning phase can come as a welcome energetic break from the intense lunar energies. This makes the Waning Gibbous Moon a good time for magick associated with decrease, banishing, repelling, cleansing away negativity, and well as breaking hexes and curses. Making moon water is generally associated with the Full Moon, but it can also be made at other lunar phases, giving the water different magickal properties. Moon water made at the Waning Gibbous Moon can be used in the workings above which are associated with decrease.

Thus far, the Moon has encouraged us to refine our outward actions to manifest our intentions. Now, the waning half of the lunar cycle provides a time to go inward and reflect honestly on your feelings and the things in your life that no longer support your higher purpose. If you want to undo, destroy, or let go of any kind of unwanted energy or force in your life, like addiction, regret, guilt, and negative thinking, now is the time. This could be something as simple as writing down the things you want to release, burning them in the flame of a black candle and then burying the ashes away from your home or property.

This phase emphasizes the need to reflect on the Full Moon and what was manifested. If some of your intentions did bear fruit, this phase encourages gratitude for the things that you have achieved. This phase of the Moon is known as a "disseminating Moon" which speaks about the importance of sharing the fruits of your labor in order to help others. It's possible that not all your goals were manifested during the Full Moon, so take the Waning Gibbous Moon as an opportunity to re-evaluate your intentions and assess why they did not come into being. The push to look inward provides the chance to reflect on the things that are blocking you from accomplishing your goals. Re-adjust and make the changes you need so you can refocus your intentions for the rest of the lunar cycle and consider how you plan to achieve your goals.

LAST QUARTER
Day 21

At the Last (or Third) Quarter, the Moon is at half power and only illuminated on the left-hand side. Light and dark are equal and it's another reminder of the importance of balance within our lives for our wellbeing. Look inward to the areas of your life that feel out of balance and connect with the lunar energies to help you assess what you need to do to restore your sense of equilibrium. Part of restoring the balance is learning when to slow down. At this phase of the cycle, the Moon's energy is decreasing, so you may feel your personal energies are lower than usual. View this as Mother Nature's way of trying to slow you down to enable you to complete this lunar cycle, but also prepare you for the next since, like the Wheel of the Year, the lunar cycle never stops.

The best kind of magick to perform at this Moon phase is similar to that of the magick associated with the Waning Gibbous Moon: decreasing, banishing, binding, and deep cleansing. Now is time let go and release anything you are still holding on to that stands in the way of you accomplishing your goals. The Waning Gibbous Moon provided an opportunity to let go of these things, now the Last Quarter asks you to look inward again and release any blockages that remain. It could be something like breaking a bad habit, learning not to be a push-over or walking away from any kind of toxic person or situation that drains and unbalances your personal energy. It's time to push aside obstacles to make a clear path forward for yourself.

The lunar cycle is almost complete but before the New Moon arrives, the Last Quarter encourages a time of introspection. It's a time to look back on all you've achieved and accomplished and reflect on the lessons the Moon has taught you over the last cycle. If you are searching for what these lessons might mean, you are more likely to gain a deeper level of understanding at this Moon phase. This makes the Last Quarter the best time for completing any personal developmental work such as finally work letting go of any self-limiting beliefs, or fears that stop you moving forward. All the inner work you have been doing will help you to form your intentions and set your goals for the next lunar cycle.

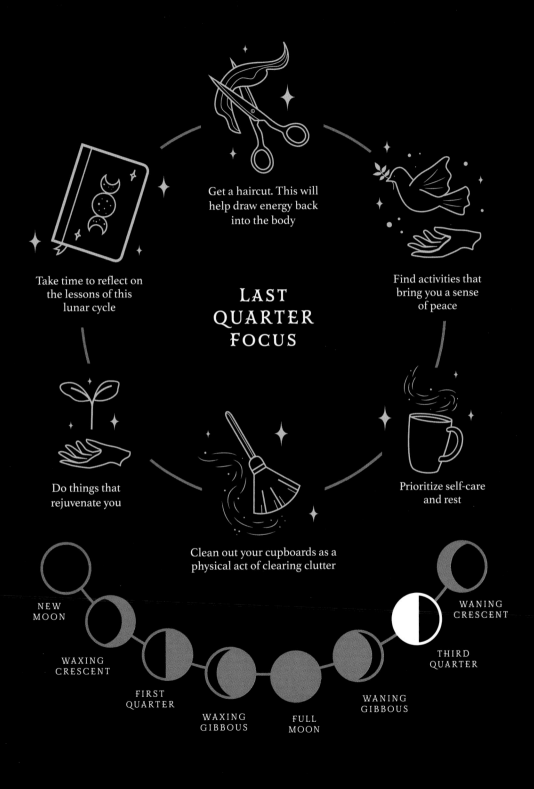

Get a haircut. This will help draw energy back into the body

Find activities that bring you a sense of peace

Prioritize self-care and rest

Clean out your cupboards as a physical act of clearing clutter

Do things that rejuvenate you

Take time to reflect on the lessons of this lunar cycle

LAST
QUARTER
FOCUS

NEW
MOON

WAXING
CRESCENT

FIRST
QUARTER

WAXING
GIBBOUS

FULL
MOON

WANING
GIBBOUS

THIRD
QUARTER

WANING
CRESCENT

WANING CRESCENT
Day 25

This is the final phase of the lunar cycle, where only a small piece of the left-hand side of the Moon is illuminated and is most visible before Sunrise. As the energy of the Moon is still decreasing at the Waning Crescent Moon, your personal energy levels are still likely to be affected. It's a reminder that in order to begin a brand-new lunar cycle at the New Moon, resting is a necessary step to completing the old cycle. This phase is a time for self-care, self-kindness, and self-forgiveness. Don't be tempted to overwork, but instead focus on activities that recharge your batteries and give you a sense of rejuvenation and peace rather than things that will be a drain on your energy. Rest is an important ritual in itself and can often be forgotten in the busyness of our daily lives.

There is a degree of surrendering to what has been at the Waning Crescent Moon. What has passed during this lunar phase is now firmly rooted in the past where nothing can be done to change it. It's a reminder that we don't always have control in life, and that's ok! Sometimes the greatest freedom can be found in those moments where we simply trust and surrender to something greater, whether that be a deity, the universe, or the force of nature itself. This last Moon phase before the New Moon is the time to prepare yourself for a new lunar cycle by giving yourself permission to wind down and rest for a while. You may find it beneficial to use this time to detach from the world for a while so you can truly rest, clear space for what is to come, and find a greater sense of inner balance. This makes meditation and journaling good activities to practice at the Waning Crescent Moon.

The Waning Crescent Moon is our last chance to let go of anything that doesn't align with our higher purpose before we start a new lunar cycle. If any of your intentions or goals didn't manifest, don't be too hard on yourself as you can reflect more on why this might have been so. By the start of the next lunar cycle, your intentions are more focused and refined. Like the other phases of the waning half of the Moon cycle, this phase is associated with banishing and decrease, particularly if there is something you want to cut out of your life completely.

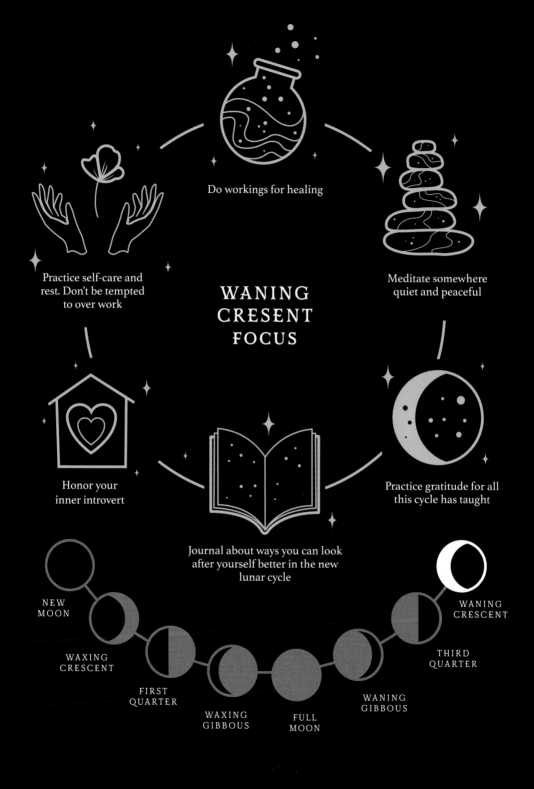

Do workings for healing

Meditate somewhere
quiet and peaceful

Practice self-care and
rest. Don't be tempted
to over work

WANING
CRESENT
FOCUS

Practice gratitude for all
this cycle has taught

Honor your
inner introvert

Journal about ways you can look
after yourself better in the new
lunar cycle

NEW
MOON

WANING
CRESCENT

WAXING
CRESCENT

THIRD
QUARTER

FIRST
QUARTER

WANING
GIBBOUS

WAXING
GIBBOUS

FULL
MOON

Let your
desires and
goals be
known

4

SPELLS

Casting a spell can help you focus on what you really want from life, whether that is drawing money, protection, happiness or love toward you, or removing unwanted things from your life such as negative energy or obstacles. Spellwork and magick play a central role in our Craft, and are ways of deepening our connection to the natural world, because it is from the natural world that we draw much of our energy and power. When we align our spells with the phase of the Moon or use herbs that best correspond with our specific intentions, this is natural magick.

The tools provided in this chapter will enable you to cast spells using colors, candles, herbs, and sigils, as well as show you how to make substitutions in your workings and how to pick the best time of day for your spells to ensure the highest chance of success. The guidance in this chapter will also help you to make any spell written by another your own.

Self-doubt can kill any spell.
If you have doubts it will
work, it probably won't.

You cast the spell too early
without doing the necessary
reading and research.

You cast a spell that was too
big or complicated.

You are casting a spell when
you are tired, ill, or not in
the right headspace.

The spell goes against your
own morals so you are
battling with your mind.

You are not doing the
mundane work to achieve
your goals.

You used ingredients that
contradict or go against
your intentions.

You have expectations for
your spell that are not based
on reality or aren't practical.

You use a spell someone
else has written that doesn't
quite meet your goals.

Your intentions are
not focused and
specific enough.

You have focused on the
things you don't want rather
than what you do want.

You rely on just having
the right ingredients to
make your spell work.

SPELL CASTING
Common Mistakes

When it comes to casting spells, the truth is they don't always work. There are many reasons why this could be, and it doesn't only happen for those at the beginning of their Witchcraft journey.

The most common reason why a spell doesn't work is that the practitioner's intention isn't specific enough. One of the most important things when casting a spell is to focus on a clear and definitive goal. Defining your exact intention can be difficult but the secret is to not rush the process. Take your time to develop your intentions before you cast the spell, so you have the space to keep refining them. The more specific your intentions are, the better your chance of success.

If we want our spells to be effective, we must be ready to put in the mundane work. Our magick must always be supported by our actions and thoughts so we can do all that's possible to achieve our goals. For example, if you were to cast a spell to help you in an important exam, you wouldn't just turn up to take the exam without revising beforehand, hoping the spell will somehow get you through. Having unrealistic expectations will almost certainly see your spell fail, as would a lack of preparation. While Witchcraft allows us to make changes to our environment, spells that seem too good to be true almost certainly are. Your goals must be rooted in reality to be successful and you must be committed to playing your part too. It is also not enough to simply use the right ingredients in a spell—you must also have the passion and intention to make it a success.

Self-doubt can make the most precise spell fail. If you have any doubts in your magickal ability or in the spell itself, it's almost certain not to work. You must believe in yourself and your power. Just because a spell doesn't work instantly, doesn't mean it isn't having an effect. Casting doubt upon the spell afterward can also have a negative effect on the outcome. Once you have cast your spell, the best approach is to try your best to forget it. You've let your desires and goals be known, now let the source of power you called upon do its part as you continue to do the mundane work.

TYPES OF SPELLS

CANDLE
The most accessible magick for
beginners, burn a candle in the color
that matches your intention.

SPRAY
An easy burst of magick on
the go made with herbs or
essential oils.

JAR
Jars concentrate the energy
of your spell in one place for
extra power.

TYPES OF
Spells

Spell-work is the action of raising, directing, and manipulating energy to either control or bring about subtle change to our environment, which allows us to achieve our goals. There are many kinds of spells and many ways to perform them. The different spells covered here will explain the basics of what they are and how to make your own. All the spells here can be made for any purpose, so get creative!

Sprays

Sprays are a good way to bring a burst of magick to life exactly when you need it. You can use essential oils in water for a quick and easy spray, or you can add herbs too. One way is to put your herbs in a pan full of water, bring them to a boil on the stove and then let them simmer on a medium heat for 3-5 minutes before letting the water cool. This allows time for the natural oils in the herbs to seep out. Once the water is completely cool, pour into a spray bottle, and it is ready to use. Alternatively, add herbs to water and leave them in the bottle to infuse gradually. The spray will last for about 2 weeks before the herbs become moldy. Use moon water for the spray to give it extra power.

Jars

Jar/bottle spells are easy to make. They concentrate the magickal energy of a spell in a physical container to make it more powerful. They can be created by including herbs, crystals, and any other items that align with the intention of your spell. I recommend you use dried ingredients because after the bottle is filled, it should be fully sealed with wax, so contents won't become moldy. With this in mind, make sure all herbs are fully dried before using. When the jar is made up, choose a colored candle that aligns with the intention of your spell, light it, and then drip the hot wax on top of the bottle to seal. I use spell jars for home protection, where I've hung one above my front and back doors. I use equal parts of fennel, yarrow, rosemary, cinnamon, and lavender then seal it with the wax of a black candle.

Candles

One of the most accessible and simple forms of magick, you will learn more about candle magick on page 101.

Oil blends

Oil blends can be made in two ways. The first method is to use a carrier oil like grape or vegetable oil for the base, and then add a blend of essential oils. Using a light oil as a carrier, as well as food-grade essential oil, means the mix won't be too concentrated or irritating if used on the skin. Make sure the essential oils you use have the properties that support your intentions, and that you avoid ingesting or making skin contact with essential oils if you have sensitive skin, any allergies or health conditions, or are pregnant, unless approved by your health practitioner. The second method is to use a base oil as before, and place fresh or dried herbs directly into the oil and leave it for a few weeks (or a few months if you want a super concentrated oil). Stir the mix well every few days and as you do, focus on the intention of the spell. If it's a spell to increase something, like protection, stir it clockwise (deosil) and if it's a spell for decrease, stir it anti-clockwise (widdershins). When it's ready, drain out the herbs and pour it into a rollerball bottle to make it easier and less messy to carry and use.

Pouches

Pouches and sachets are made in a similar way to jars, using ingredients dried to prevent mold. Although the pouch concentrates the energy of your spell within it like a jar, it's still able to exchange energy with its environment as the bag is porous unlike glass. To finish the sachet, tie it with a ribbon in a corresponding color to the intent of your spell. I use them when a spell calls for me to carry the ingredients used with me throughout my day, such as a protection spell, but I have also used them for sleep spells, putting the herbs and crystals I used under my pillow. Generally, after the spell is complete, the pouch is returned to Earth and buried, so if you choose to bury your pouch, try and make the ingredients you use are biodegradable.

Potions

Potions are liquid spells made to be consumed internally or applied externally to the body. A potion could be a tincture, perfume, or your favorite drink. Tea is a popular potion, which is a good way to benefit from the medicinal properties of the herbs you use. You can charge your morning cup of tea (or any drink) by meditating on the cup and sending your intention to charge it. When you feel you've charged it enough, drink it. You can also trace the shape of a pentacle over your drink for protection. Tracing around the rim of the cup clockwise for a potion associated with increase and anti-clockwise for one associated with decrease is another way to charge your potions.

TYPES OF SPELLS

OILS
Made from a base or carrier oil and a blend of essential oils or herbs left to infuse the base.

POUCHES
Pouches contain the spell's energy similar to a jar spell. Use a ribbon to tie the pouch.

POTIONS
Potions are liquid spells that are consumed or put externally on the body.

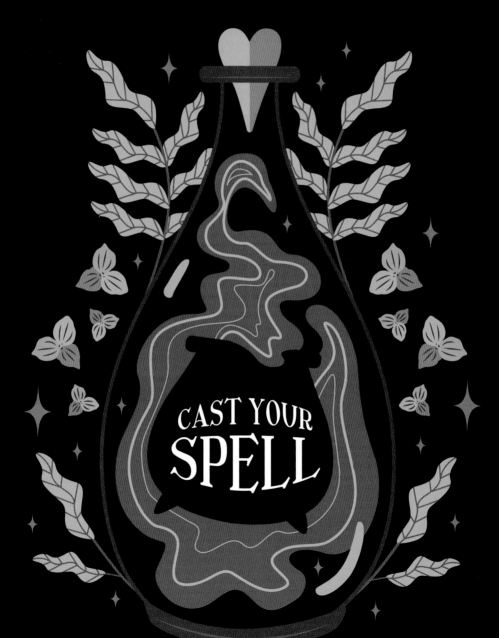

SPELL
Crafting

When it comes to spells, the ones you write yourself hold more power, although using a spell written by someone else might work well. When I create my spells, I find it helpful to go through this practical check list to know I have everything ready.

Intention

What is your aim for your spell? What actions do you need to put in place in your wider life to support your goals? Your intentions need to be as specific and focused as possible.

Who

Be clear about who your spell is aimed at—is it yourself or someone else? How will it affect them/you?

Location

Where are you planning to cast your spell? Outside or inside? You need to be able to give your spell your full attention, so make sure you at ease with your environment.

Tools/materials

What materials do you need to cast your spell? For example, do you need candles or herbs? And if so, which colors or herbs will align with your overall intention for the spell. List everything you are likely to need; there's nothing more distracting than getting halfway through your spell and realizing you need to go and fetch something you've forgotten.

Time

Refer to Spell Timings on page 96 for more information.

Casting

When you're ready to cast your spell, go through your list to make sure you've remembered everything. Use this as a time to check in with yourself on both a physical and spiritual level to make sure you are ready to cast your spell.

Disposing of your spells

There are different ways to dispose of the remnants of a spell. As a rule, I don't throw away spell ingredients. There are some exceptions such as throwing away the remnants of a banishing spell or one cast to absorb negativity. But in general, leftovers are returned to Earth by burying them. Remember not to bury salt as it will kill anything it comes into contact with (you can flush or throw it away instead). Avoid burying non-biodegradable ingredients. Things like wax, string, cords, paper, or fabric can also be disposed of using fire.

SPELL
Timings

In Witchcraft, if we align our spells to the corresponding time and day, it can help to increase its chance of success. Correspondences are used in the Craft to enhance the efficiency of your working. They are lists of the magickal properties associated with physical items such as herbs, flowers, crystals, and incense, and also for things like timings, such as the magick associated with the different Moon phases.

The time of the day and different days of the week are also connected with different kinds of magick, and aligning the intentions of your spell with the right times can help to give your workings a boost of energy. Although timing alone is not essential to a spell's efficiency (casting a spell that isn't aligned with the most suitable time isn't enough to cause a spell to fail), it is still an important consideration that can help boost your spell-work.

Correspondences associated with the times of the day:
SUNRISE—NEW beginnings, fresh energies, travel, cleansing, purifying, healing, study, initiative

DAYTIME—EXPANSION, intelligence, leadership, conscious mind

MIDDAY—POWER, health, money, success, strength, protection, opportunity, vitality

SUNSET—FINDING truth, release, letting go, banishing, breaking bad habits, closure

NIGHT-TIME—INVENTING, self-development, awareness, releasing stress/worry, healing old wounds

MIDNIGHT—BANISHING, divination, healing, self-enhancement

The days of the week are all dedicated to an ancient Greek or Roman deity, each with their corresponding planet. It is the planet that gives the days of the week their names but also their magickal properties.

Days of the week:
MONDAY—RULED by deities Selene/Luna and the Moon

TUESDAY—RULED by deities Ares/Mars the planet Mars

WEDNESDAY—RULED by deities Hermes/Mercury and the planet Mercury

THURSDAY—RULED by deities Zeus/Jupiter and the planet Jupiter

FRIDAY—RULED by deities Aphrodite/Venus and the planet Venus

SATURDAY—RULED by deities Cronus/Saturn and the planet Saturn

SUNDAY—RULED by deities Apollo/Sol and the Sun

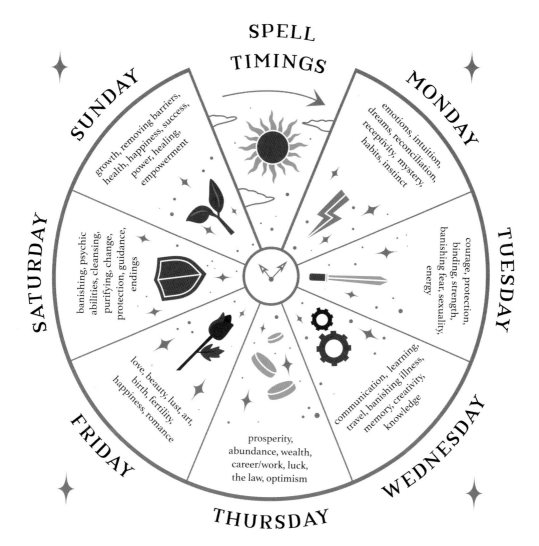

SPELL TIMINGS

SUNDAY
growth, removing barriers, health, happiness, success, power, healing, empowerment

MONDAY
emotions, intuition, dreams, reconciliation, receptivity, mystery, habits, instinct

SATURDAY
banishing, psychic abilities, cleansing, purifying, change, protection, guidance, endings

TUESDAY
courage, protection, binding, strength, banishing fear, sexuality, energy

FRIDAY
love, beauty, lust, art, birth, fertility, happiness, romance

WEDNESDAY
communication, learning, travel, banishing illness, memory, creativity, knowledge

THURSDAY
prosperity, abundance, wealth, career/work, luck, the law, optimism

COLOR *Magick*

Every color on the spectrum vibrates at its own specific frequency and represents a different set of magickal qualities. Color magick uses the energies and vibrations in magickal workings to bring about the changes you want to see. It can easily be incorporated into your Craft and learning the basics can help to give your spells and rituals an extra boost of power. It can be as simple as wearing something orange to give you confidence in a job interview or burning a purple candle when you are practicing divination to help connect with your psychic abilities. Color magick is also a subtle way of practicing your Craft, so it's great for those in the broom closet. You can incorporate color magick into your life discreetly in many ways:

+✦ Wear the color that supports your spell.
+✦ Adapt the color of your make-up or nail polish.
+✦ Write in a colored pen that suits your needs.
+✦ Sew, embroider, or knit using the color thread that aligns with your intentions.
+✦ Buy flowers in the color aligned with your intention and put them in your home/space.
+✦ Use a colored cup that best suits your needs and drink from it.

+✦ Take a ritual bath using a colored bath bomb or bubble bath that best aligns with your intentions.

The correspondences we use in the Craft today (including color but also any other kind of materials and ingredients you might use such as herbs, crystals, and incense) are generally influenced by and originate from ancient occult texts. The magickal properties or correspondences associated with every color have in part come from these older sources, but they have also been culturally influenced over the centuries too. These are only general correspondences but as you grow as a Witch and explore more of the Craft, you may come to find that you build up your own set of magickal properties associated with every kind of ingredient and material you use in your rituals and spells.

As you expand your magickal experience and knowledge, let your intuition guide you as to what you feel works best for you. For example, orange is the traditional color of creativity, but over the years, I've found that orange seems to sap my creative abilities, but blue helps me to access my creativity far more easily.

WHITE: Purification, cleansing, protection, healing
BLACK: Acceptance, banishing, binding, break curses and hexes
BROWN: Earth, grounding, healing, endurance, stability
PINK: Acceptance, romance, compassion, family, sensuality
RED: Courage, assertiveness, energy, passion, power, action
ORANGE: Abundance, ambition, happiness, confidence, creativity
YELLOW: Action, joy, communication, enthusiasm, abundance
GREEN: Acceptance, action, agriculture, change, harmony, luck
PURPLE: Astrology, intuition, enlightenment, psychic protection
BLUE: Honesty, communication, self-expression, healing, peace
SILVER: Awareness, intuition, Moon, purification, feminine energy
GOLD: Abundance, influence, luxury, masculine energy, Sun magick

SHINE YOUR LIGHT AND BURN BRIGHT

CANDLE
Magick

Candle magick is one of the easiest ways to incorporate magick into your life. If you're just starting your Witchcraft journey, it's a great introduction to spell-work. It's also inexpensive, meaning it's a good form of magick for the Witch on budget. Candle magick represents all four elements and blends all them together in a sort of alchemy, which harnesses the very power of nature to bring about the change we want. The flame of the candle represents Fire, the melted wax represents Water, the candle needs Air to burn, and Earth is represented by the solid wax.

When performing candle magick there are a few things to consider before you begin. A candle spell can be as simple as blessing and lighting a candle with intention, but there are other options to give your spell a natural boost of energy. The first place to start is to choose a colored candle that best aligns with your goals and intentions for the spell. For example, for a protective spell, a black candle would be the best choice.

You can also add power to your workings by aligning the intentions of your spell with the right day of the week, the time of day and the corresponding Moon phase. These things alone will not cause your spell to fail if you can't align all the times, but if you can, it will certainly add more strength and energy to your workings. The same is true for herbs and crystals and any sigils (see Chapter 6) you wish to carve into the wax: choosing the ones that also support your intentions will help to give your spell a natural energetic boost. To dress a candle, rub an oil like olive or vegetable over the candle either in a clockwise (increase) or anti-clockwise (decrease) direction and then roll it in roughly ground up herbs of your choice.

Candle size is another consideration. Some spells require the candle to burn out to complete the spell, so for these spells you might need a smaller candle, so it doesn't take a long time to burn away. On the other hand, you might need your candle to burn for a few hours every day for a week, so these spells require a larger candle.

Candle burn time:
BIRTHDAY–2–5 minutes
CHIME–2–2.5 hours
TEALIGHT–2–2.5 hours
VOTIVE–6–7 hours
TAPER–9–10 hours

Remember to never leave candles burning unattended.

 # SUBSTITUTIONS
in Spell-work

Magickal substitution is the act of replacing one ingredient in a spell with another, usually because the spell calls for an ingredient we don't have. It's fairly common to come across a spell that requires an obscure herb or a candle on a color we don't have. This doesn't have to be a problem because there are several general substitutions you can make within your spell-work which can open up more magickal possibilities. Many of these substitute ingredients are also budget friendly and are readily available.

Rosemary, white candles and clear quartz are fantastic items to have because they are so versatile. Respectively, they can replace any herb, any colored candle and any crystal within your spells, so are useful items to have in your store cupboard. The great thing about rosemary is that it can be used fresh or dried, and it is a herb that you are likely to already have in your kitchen cupboard or even grow in your garden. This is helpful for those in the broom closet who may not be able to get hold of specific ingredients but are more likely to have access to herbs like rosemary.

It's also easy to grow outdoors—plant rosemary in spring or autumn in sandy, well-drained soil where it can get lots of sun.

These substitutions are only general and while they can be substituted for anything in their separate categories (herbs, candles, crystals, salt, flowers, and so on,) it doesn't make them the best ingredient for the job. As each color has its own set of correspondences, so do the ingredients in each category, so to make the best substitution, it's a good idea to match the correspondence of the item you want to use as a substitution with the intention of your spell. For example, rosemary is a protective herb so would be a good substitute for any herb in a protection spell but would be less effective to use as a substitute in a money spell. Intention-based substitutions are more likely to yield success as you are making sure that all the items you use are in alignment with your overall goals and intentions for your spell. General substitutions are good if you need to cast a spell and you don't have another option.

SUBSTITUTIONS IN SPELL-WORK

Rosemary replaces
any herb

White candles replace
any colored candles

Rose replaces
any flower

Clear quartz replaces
any crystals

Lemon replaces
any citrus

Black tea replaces any
tea blend

Tabacco replaces any
toxic herb

Frankincense replaces
any resin

Olive oil replaces any oil/
carrier oil

Table salt replaces
any salt

Apple replaces
any fruit

Naga champa (flower)
replaces any incense

REWORKING
Spells

Reworking a spell goes hand in glove with making substitutions. It means taking a prewritten spell and using it as a base but making changes to better suit your needs and situation. Reworking is a common process and could include making changes to the words, actions and ingredients of a spell or any references to a deity. You can rework any part of a spell that either doesn't align with your intentions or doesn't feel right to you and your own particular practice.

There are many reasons why you would choose to rework a spell and there are many specific areas within a working that might need to be changed. For example, you might choose to make changes to a spell because you are unable to light a candle or burn incense in your home so need alternatives. Luckily, there are things you can still do. Battery or LED candles are a good option, and to bring in the use of color, you can stick washi tape in the color most aligned with the intentions of your spell on them. You could also include unlit candles in a color that supports the intention of your spell but use visualization to harness the energy they contain.

A spell may call for you to burn something such as paper or herbs, and this might not be a viable option for you. So, it's crucial you use alternative actions that have the same energetic effect as burning such as cutting with scissors,

shredding, or tearing. This will help to increase the spell's chance of success. It's important that whatever reworking you do, any changes you make do not change the overall energy of the original spell. Keep all your reworkings intention-based so you are sure you are replacing any actions, words, and gestures with those of similar energies. There are also alternatives to speaking or chanting and ingestion. We may find ourselves in a position where we are unable to speak the words of a spell out loud, particularly those in the broom closet, but you could write the spell down or speak the words aloud in your head. If a spell calls for you to drink something you would rather not, tipping some onto the ground is a good alternative action. Any restrictions that are based on your personal circumstances do not place a limit on your magick if you look for alternative routes that will lead you to the same results.

PROTECTION *Spell*

Of all the kinds of spells I get asked for, protection spells are the most popular, so I wanted to share this protection spell from my Grimoire. It's a simple candle spell that can be used to protect yourself from any kind of negative energy or force, and can also be cast on behalf of someone else. As a protection spell, it is best cast on the Full or Waxing Moon.

Ingredients
Three black candles.
Red candle.
Black Tourmaline.
Black Obsidian.
Sea salt.
Bay leaves.
Rosemary.
Black pepper.
Vervain.
Olive oil.
Small bottle/pouch.
Catnip, frankincense & myrrh incense, wine (offerings).
Mortar & pestle

If you don't have some of these ingredients, see page 103 to see what substitutions you can make.

After cleansing myself and my space, I call upon the elements for extra power. It also helps me to connect with nature's energy not just in this spell, but also in my wider practice. I don't often work with deities, but for this spell, I chose to invoke the Egyptian Goddess of Protection, Bastet, but you can work with whatever deity feels right to you. You don't even have to work with a deity. These are the words I used but feel free to rework this spell using the wording that feels most authentic to you.

The idea for this spell was to create a protective jar you could keep with you or keep inside your home. If you don't have a bottle. you can put the ingredients in a black pouch. I use the colored pouches that often come with jewelry as they are the perfect size. The spell calls for three black candles for protection and one red candle to represent Bastet, but if this is difficult, you could use white for all.

Black tourmaline helps to create a protective shield, and black obsidian is used for protection and to reverse curses, hexes and psychic attacks.

Fill the bottle/pouch while focusing on your intention for the spell. Once the bottle is filled, seal it with the wax of a black candle, or tie the pouch with black ribbon. If it's for someone else, give them the bottle/pouch to keep.

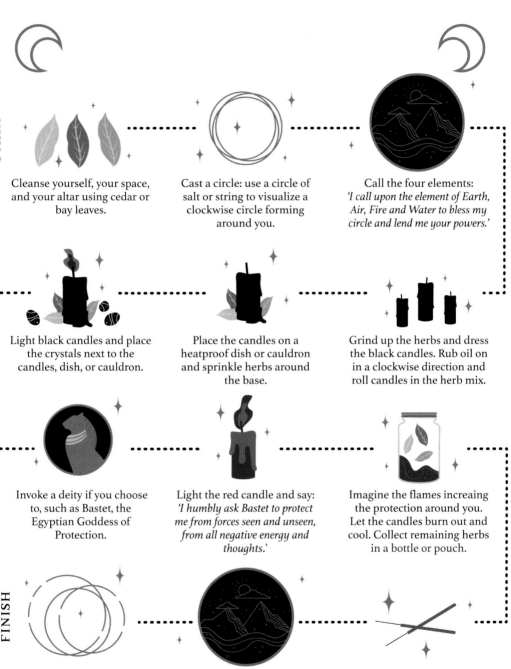

START

Cleanse yourself, your space, and your altar using cedar or bay leaves.

Cast a circle: use a circle of salt or string to visualize a clockwise circle forming around you.

Call the four elements: *'I call upon the element of Earth, Air, Fire and Water to bless my circle and lend me your powers.'*

Light black candles and place the crystals next to the candles, dish, or cauldron.

Place the candles on a heatproof dish or cauldron and sprinkle herbs around the base.

Grind up the herbs and dress the black candles. Rub oil on in a clockwise direction and roll candles in the herb mix.

Invoke a deity if you choose to, such as Bastet, the Egyptian Goddess of Protection.

Light the red candle and say: *'I humbly ask Bastet to protect me from forces seen and unseen, from all negative energy and thoughts.'*

Imagine the flames increasing the protection around you. Let the candles burn out and cool. Collect remaining herbs in a bottle or pouch.

FINISH

Visualize the energy you created being released to close your circle. Sweep up the salt or gather the string in an anti-clockwise motion.

Thank and say goodbye to the elements in the opposite order you called them.

Thank Bastet, leave offerings of wine, catnip, and frankincense and myrrh incense.

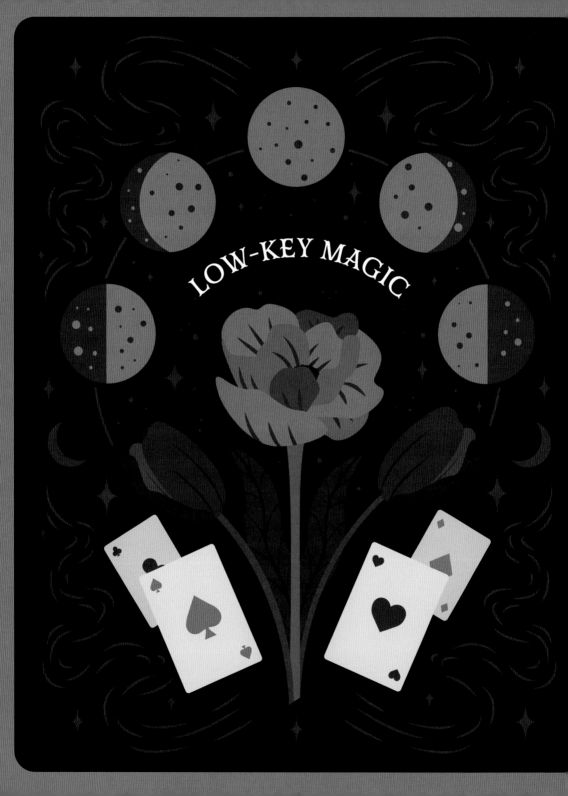

5

WITCHRAFT IN THE BROOM CLOSET

"In the broom closet" has become a well-used turn of phrase for those Witches who can't or don't want to practice their Craft openly. Witches go and stay in the broom closet for a variety of reasons. Some are there because their living situation doesn't allow them to be open, or the people in their lives would react negatively if they were honest. Others are there because they don't want people to know their personal business, and sadly, some are in situations where it would be physically dangerous to be a Witch and practice their Craft, even in this modern day. All these are valid reasons that should be respected, and they certainly don't make you any less of a Witch!

For me personally, I began my Witchcraft journey when my family's Christian beliefs meant I couldn't be open about who I was. It wasn't until my circumstances changed in 2017 that I was able to be open with everyone about my Craft, and I realized how much keeping that part of me a secret weighed upon my soul. I felt a huge weight was lifted and it felt liberating!

While being in the broom closet does have its disadvantages, it doesn't mean you can't practice your Craft! This chapter contains many tips for celebrating the Sabbats, honoring the Moon phases, subtle morning, and evening rituals and lot of general Witchy ideas and tricks for practicing your Craft in the broom closet.

Visit the graves of
loved ones.

Core pumpkins and
decorate your space.

Make a pendulum from a
necklance and pendant.

Set intentions and goals for
the new year.

SUBTLE
SABBATS:
SAMHAIN

Meditate on your growth
over the last year.

Do family research.

Go on a nature walk to
connect with the Earth.

Decorate a Yule tree
with lights.

Decorate a Yule log.

SUBTLE
SABBATS:
YULE

Watch the sunrise/sunset on
the shortest day.

Decorate your home with
lights and baubles.

Place a Yule wreath on
your front door.

SUBTLE *Sabbats*

Samhain

Samhain is the beginning of the Witches new year, so is a great time to set your intentions for the year ahead. Make some space for yourself so you can think about what you would like to achieve and how you plan to work toward your goals, so you are able to set clear intentions. This Sabbat celebrates the cycles of life and death and is a time to honor our ancestors. If you're able, visit the graves of loved ones that have passed and take time to remember them. Start to research your family history or look through old photographs as an act of remembrance and honor. Even buy a special frame for your favorite family picture.

In the secular world, Halloween is increasingly celebrated, so take advantage and decorate your space or home! Carve pumpkins to celebrate the third and final harvest of the year and even try your hand at preserving food for the winter. Samhain is associated with divination as the veil between this world and the next is at its thinnest. You can still practice divination in the broom closet, and although you may not have tarot cards, you can easily make a pendulum from a necklace and pendant and a scrying surface with a bowl of water.

Yule

When it comes to practicing the Sabbats in the broom closet, I found I had more freedom at Yule because so many traditions and activities have found their way into mainstream consciousness, and have become part of society's usual Christmas celebrations. Decorating trees with lights as well as decorating our homes with evergreens, candles, and colored baubles are common activities around Yuletide, which means these practices (which are essentially Pagan in origin) can be enjoyed as celebrations of the shortest day when in the broom closet. It's a time to take full advantage of the cultural appropriation of Pagan rites and traditions at this time of the year!

Venturing out into nature is an excellent way to celebrate each Sabbat because it's a low-key way of honoring the changing of the seasons and immersing yourself in the energies of the natural world. It's also a good way of grounding and balancing our own personal energies too, so works to give our sense of wellbeing a boost at the same time. Watching the Sun rise or set on the shortest day of the year is another way to not only celebrate the Winter Solstice and the passing of time, but also strengthen our connection with nature.

Get a houseplant or re-pot
one you already have.

Make your own candles to
welcome back the Sun.

Cinnamon magic.

SUBTLE
SABBATS:
IMBOLC

Honor Brigid: learn more
about her or write poetry.

Drink/eat dairy (or a
vegan alternative).

Cleanse and purify your
space.

Bring spring flowers inside
where you can see them.

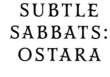

Begin plans for a
new project.

Clean your space and sweep
away bad energy.

SUBTLE
SABBATS:
OSTARA

Go on a nature walk to look
for signs of spring.

Garden or re-pot a
house plant.

Open your windows to
let the spring air in.

Imbolc

As the first fire festival of the year, you can celebrate Imbolc by lighting a candle (or many if you are able) or use battery-operated candles if you are unable to have real candles to represent the bonfires traditionally lit on this Sabbat to welcome back the Sun. Imbolc is associated with the Goddess Brigid and drinking or eating dairy products (or dairy-free vegan substitutes) and writing poetry are traditional ways to honor her. Getting a houseplant or re-potting a plant you already have can help you connect with the fertility of the soil, and is a great subtle activity you can carry out on Imbolc.

This Sabbat is a great time to get in touch with your own psychic abilities as the natural world begins to wake up. You can use cinnamon to help connect you to your senses, as cinnamon helps us to raise our psychic awareness. You can drink it in a tea, put it in food like apple pie, or burn cinnamon incense if this is possible. If none of these is doable, just have a cinnamon stick in your space so it can fragrance the room, to gently cleanse and purify.

Ostara

Spring cleaning is a fantastic Ostara activity for those in the broom closet. Not only can you physically clear and organize your space or home, but you can also visualize sweeping out any negative energy that has accumulated—and you don't need a besom to do it! Using a vacuum cleaner or dustpan and brush will do the same job as you focus your attention on removing any unwanted energies. As you clean, open all your windows to let in the fresh spring air! Celebrating the Sabbats can be done under the guise of mundane, everyday activities!

If you are green fingered, get gardening! Planting is a wonderful way to connect with the energies of the earth. You could even take off your shoes and do some grounding by walking or sitting barefoot on the earth. It can give you a boost of natural energy especially if your own energy levels are running low. If this isn't possible, purchasing, planting, or repotting a houseplant is a good way to connect to the Ostara energy of growth and fertility. A nature walk or just getting out into nature is always an option, especially if you can't do any gardening, as it gives you the option to immerse yourself in Earth's natural energies.

Beltane

As Beltane is one of the great fire festivals, celebrating the sabbat can be as simple as lighting a red, orange, or yellow candle to represent the color of the balefires that are traditionally lit at this time of year. You may not be able to light a bonfire yourself but blessing and lighting a candle can represent the same meaning. Beltane is essentially about celebrating life, so having a feast of your favorite foods or decorating your space with a simple vase of spring flowers are great ideas to celebrate this Sabbat.

Since Beltane celebrations usually occur outside, take advantage of the warmer weather and get out into nature. Go outside or take a small picnic to your favorite natural spot (mine was always in the local forest) and enjoy some springtime food like bread, cakes, honey, and seasonal vegetables. It gives you a chance to connect with the Earth at the height of her springtime energies and to appreciate new life in all its beauty. Even spending a short amount of time in nature and hearing the birds sing can help to deepen your connections with all the seasonal changes happening all around you.

Litha

Litha (or the Summer Solstice) celebrates the longest day and is the opposite Sabbat to Yule on the Wheel of the Year. Like at Yule, you can celebrate the Solstice by watching the Sun rise either from outside, or if this would raise too much suspicion, from a window inside. It's a very traditional way to honor the longest day and can be done subtly in the broom closet.

Bringing the outside in is a discreet way to honor the Sabbats. At Litha, fill a vase full of summer flowers and put them in your window to charge under the Sun on the longest day of the year. Even just one flower for symbolism helps you to connect with the Sabbat and the natural world. Being in the broom closet taught me that our rituals or activities don't have to be big or complex to be meaningful. At Litha, bonfires are lit to celebrate the power of the Sun, and while this might not be an option for many, lighting a single candle to represent a balefire (bonfire) is still a symbolic act filled with meaning.

Litha is the time where the Sun is at the peak of its power, so enjoy the summer fruits of the earth by eating foods like watermelon, grapes, and plums. You could even go fruit picking so you can pick your own strawberries.

Have a picnic outside in
your favorite nature spot.

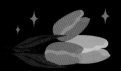

Decorate your space with
local spring flowers.

Light a red, orange, or
yellow candle to represent
a balefire.

SUBTLE
SABBATS:
BELTANE

Take a ritual bath using
spring flowers.

Plant bulbs
and flowers.

Cook your seasonal foods
for a feast.

Decorate your home with
summer flowers.

Bake honey cakes.

Light a candle to symbolize
the Sun.

Honor the longest day by
watching the the sunrise.

SUBTLE
SABBATS:
LITHA

Go on a nature walk.

Eat summer fruits like
strawberries.

Do some prosperity
workings.

Pick sunflowers. The center
represents the Sun and the
seeds symbolize fertility.

Try preserving and
canning food.

SUBTLE SABBATS: LAMMAS

Bless your home/space.

Get your garden ready
for winter.

Meditate on all that you
are spiritually harvesting
in your life.

Bake bread.

Go on a nature walk in the
woods and observe the
falling leaves.

Practice gratitude.
Make a gratitude list or
photo collage.

Give and share food with
those who need it.

SUBTLE SABBATS: MABON

Make apple pie—or
anything with apples.

Meditate on balance
outside to connect with
the seasonal changes.

Lammas (Lughnasadh)

Lammas is the first of the three harvests of the Wheel of the Year, so it's a great time to bake bread or pastries. You could also try your hand at preserving food like fruits and making jams, both traditional Lammas activities for getting ready for the winter ahead. Drink a cup of chamomile or mint tea to attract good fortune and as you drink it, trace your finger around the rim of the cup in a clockwise motion to signify increase as you seek to draw abundance toward you.

Lammas is the celebration of the middle of summer, but it's also a reminder that winter is only just around the corner. The winter months were the hardest times of all so it was traditional for Pagans and Witches to bless their homes before the difficult months began. Move from room to room and silently ask for the blessing of whatever higher power you work with (whether it's a God, Goddess, or the universe in general) to fall on each room, your home in general and those that live within.

Mabon

Mabon is the time light and dark are equal in length before the Wheel moves to the dark half of the year. It's a good time for journaling or meditating on balance, as well as reflecting on the areas of your life that need equilibrium. Mabon is also a time of gratitude for the second harvest so is a great opportunity to write a gratitude list or make a collage of photographs with all the people and memories you're grateful for. The second harvest is when all the grain has been brought in, so baking bread is a great way to honor the Sabbat by using the fruits of the harvest. Making anything with apples is a good Mabon activity as it's also the time to eat the last of the summer fruits.

Mabon is the Sabbat where its traditional to share the food with those in need. I remember taking part in harvest festival celebrations during elementary (primary) school each year (a traditional celebration for schools in the UK), where we collected canned and dried food to give to local food banks. Look in your kitchen closets to see what food you could donate to those who are less fortunate.

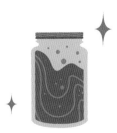

MOON
Magick

Being in the broom closet doesn't have to prevent you from honoring and connecting with each phase of the Moon, and using it as a powerful tool for change and manifestation. Moon magick doesn't have to be complicated and there are so many simple rituals and activities that can be practiced subtly and under the radar. You can still follow the rhythms of the Moon in the broom closet and embrace the power and energy of each phase.

Moon journal

Intentions can still be set at the new Moon and the other Moon phases can be used to work toward your goals. Starting a Moon journal is a good way of recording your intentions and how they are manifested gradually over time. A journal is also great for recording your feelings at each Moon phase and keeping track of how the rhythms of the Moon has an impact on your emotions, so over time, you can see any patterns that emerge.

Dream journal

A dream journal is another good tool. Record all you remember from your dreams (feelings, images, symbols, and colors), particularly around the Full Moon. Recording your dreams at different points of the lunar cycle helps you to see how the Moon affects your dreams and any

messages you receive. If there is a specific question you would like an answer to, write it in your journal before you go to sleep and it could help you find answers.

Cleanse with water

The pull of the Moon controls the tides here on Earth, so a great way to connect to the energy of the Moon is through water. Be near a lake or river on the day the phase is in alignment with your needs and any intentions. At home, fill a glass or bowl with water and use it as a meditation aid. You can still make moon water while in the broom closet. Placing a glass/jar of water on a windowsill for a few hours to absorb the Full Moon's energy can be done subtly and it doesn't need to be put outside to be fully charged. The Full Moon is also a time for cleansing and purifying, making it the perfect time to have a cleansing ritual salt bath to remove any unwanted or negative energies. You probably already have salt in your kitchen!

Water divination

Water can be used to make an easy and accessible divination tool. Many divination methods are not possible for a lot of Witches in the broom closet, but water in a bowl makes a perfect surface for scrying. which is also not overtly Witchy! Scrying is the act of looking into

Keep a
Moon journal

Visualization
and meditation

Keep a
dream journal

MOON MAGICK
IN THE
BROOM CLOSET

Try water scrying with
a bowl full of water

At the Full Moon, wrtie a
list of regrets on a piece
of paper and burn it

Look at the Moon and try to feel
her power. Feel it entering then
flowing through you

a reflective surface to make out messages and meaning. The word "scrying" comes from the Old English word "descry" which means "to make out dimly", meaning scrying is about revealing the unseen and the unknown.

Look at the surface of the water with a soft gaze so you keep your eyes as relaxed as possible. The more you relax and look, the more you tune into your second sight and it's then that you can receive images and massages.

Written rituals

There are many rituals that help you connect with the New Moon. Write down on a piece of paper all those things you want to remove or banish from your life such as bad habits, negative thinking, or unhealthy thought patterns, and then burn the paper to release the spell. If you are unable to burn the paper, then either ripping or cutting it up into small pieces and throwing it away will have the same energetic effect. You could do a similar ritual on the Full Moon by burning or tearing a list of any regrets you carry that are stopping you move forward. Connecting with the Moon in this way at both these phases can be powerful catalysts for change. Although these rituals seem very simple, they have the potential to yield powerful results if done right.

Get clarity

Visualization and meditation are useful tools to have, particularly in the broom closet, as not only will they help you focus during spells and rituals, but they can also help to align you with any phase of the Moon. It's a low-key form of Witchcraft and no tools are needed except the strength of your mind. Always decide exactly what you want to focus on before you begin and which Moon phase best corresponds to your needs. Sit somewhere comfortable where the Moon can be seen and visualize the thing you want as if it's already a reality. See and feel with all of your senses as the more detailed and your visualizations, the more precise energy you are directing at your intentions. Don't worry if at first you find meditation and visualization difficult and your mind drifts off. If this happens, just recenter and refocus yourself. It's a skill that gets easier with practice and perseverance.

Have a Moon bath;
sit in the light of
the Full Moon

Make Moon
water

Bake Moon
cakes

MOON MAGICK
IN THE
BROOM CLOSET

On the New Moon,
take some time for
grounding

On the Full Moon have a
ritual salt bath for
purification

On the New Moon, write down
what you want to banish on
paper and burn it

Make a small portable altar in a box that's easily hidden.

SUBTLE WITCHCRAFT

Connect with nature.

Grow your own kitchen herbs.

If you are able to use incense, make black salt from the ashes.

Use playing cards as tarot cards.

Draw a sigil that aligns with your intentions and keep it in your phone case.

When you move the clasp on your necklace to the back of your neck, make a wish.

Re-use and repurpose items such as jars and bottles.

Dry, press, and keep herbs in the pages of a book.

Light candles when you bathe to give you a safe place to do candle magick.

Use everyday objects such as a ring or necklace as a charm.

Use the ingredients around you, such as salt from your kitchen and dandelions from your yard.

Make the most of technology to learn and connect with other Witches.

SUBTLE
Witchcraft Tips

When in the broom closet, it can be hard to build elements of your Craft into your daily life without being too open and obvious with your actions. This can be even harder if you're also at the beginning of your Witchcraft journey. I personally found it was a balancing act between two opposing feelings; wanting my Craft to remain a secret from those around me, but still having the innate desire to express myself fully and not hide the Witch I was. But it's fair to say that telling family and friends about your practice isn't everyone's goal. Over the years of having to hide my magick, it's surprising how many ways I found that enabled me to strike a balance between honoring who I truly was while still allowing me to practice my Craft in ways that wouldn't create arguments.

If you have a pack of playing cards, you can use them as tarot cards. Tarot reading need not be a divination practice out of your reach simply because you're in the broom closet. Each playing card in the deck corresponds to a different card from the Minor Arcana (see Chapter 8 for more details) and can be used for a range of readings. This is a very discreet way to practice divination and you might even already have a pack of cards put away somewhere that you can start using.

Connecting with nature is an easy way to practice your Craft and it can be done in many ways. Going into nature can help ground and center you and help you connect to the rhythm of the seasons. You could make an altar in a small box or tin containing things like a tea light, matches, stones or rocks you've picked up along the way, or some salt in a bottle—anything you want to use and can fit in a small space that's easily put away and hidden.

You may not be able to keep jars full of herbs, but you can dry, press, and keep herbs in the pages of a book with a weight on top. Growing your own common kitchen herbs like basil, rosemary, thyme, and mint for use in "cooking" is not only a good way to physically connect with Mother Nature when you plant and tend to them, but it gives you a good source of herbs for a variety of magickal purposes. They can either be grown outside or inside in small pots and can even be bought from most supermarkets.

MORNING
Rituals

While in the broom closet, I discovered the huge value of small rituals, particularly in the morning and evening, because more complicated activities and workings were not an option. Actions like drawing a pentacle over your morning drink for protection and lighting a tealight to help you focus and set your intentions for the new day may be very simple and discreet, but they can also be very powerful. Drawing sigils that align with your goals on the labels of your clothes you want to wear or put on a piece of jewelry such as a necklace or ring that you have charmed are two other simple yet powerful ways to take your magick with you throughout the day.

You can build some time for divination and astrology into your morning routine by downloading one of the many free apps where you can read your daily horoscope. Look at the many free tarot reading apps out there too as some let you "pull" daily cards and provide card meanings. Or, if you have a deck of playing cards, as already mentioned you can use them as tarot cards; pull one each morning to give you guidance about the day ahead. You can use the mundane act of taking a morning shower and turn it into an opportunity for cleansing and protection. Visualize the water cleansing you of any negative or unwelcome energies and replacing it with its protection.

Making time to ground myself in nature is something I try to do each morning, usually in my back yard with my first cup of coffee if the weather is fair. If it's warm enough, I'll go out barefoot. The chance to connect with nature, even for just for 5 minutes, can bring so many benefits on a spiritual and emotional level. If you usually exercise in the morning, move any exercise from inside to outside. Rather than a trip to the gym, try a run outside and get some fresh air too!

MORNING RITUALS

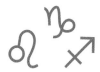

Light a candle and set your intentions for the day.

Stir your drink clockwise for increase or anti-clockwise for decrease.

Draw a sigil that aligns with your intentions on paper and keep it in your phone case.

Draw sigils on the labels of your clothes.

Write down your affirmation for the day.

Stand on some grass or earth barefoot.

Use playing cards as a tarot deck and pull a card for guidance at the beginning of the day.

Take gentle exercise like yoga to stretch out and ground yourself.

Download a horoscope app and read what the day has in store.

When you shower, visualize the water cleansing and protecting.

Trace a pentagram over your morning drink for protection.

Meditate for 5–10 minutes on your daily goals and intentions.

Tend to your houseplants.

EVENING
RITUALS

Put a beauty charm on products like face wash, moisturizer, and cleanser.

Cleanse yourself from the energies of the day.

Stir your drink clockwise for increase or anti-clockwise for decrease.

Light a lavender incense stick. They are increasingly seen as mainstream.

Start a manifestation journal on the things you're working on.

Head outside for a little grounding or open your window to let in some air.

Drink a relaxing herbal tea like chamomile.

Do some meditation and breath work.

Have a ritual bath with lavender bubble bath.

Draw a playing card to get insight on your day.

Practice gratitude for the good things about your day.

EVENING *Rituals*

Evening rituals tend to be ones that help you wind down after the activities of the day. It's a chance to relax as well as reflect on what has been and look to the day that's to come. There are lots of options open to you, but here are just a few of my nightly favorites.

Many people like to read before bed, so the evening is a great opportunity to download an e-book about Witchcraft and do some research and reading about an aspect of the Craft that interests you. Learning is a big aspect of our practice but being in the broom closet doesn't need to be a barrier between you and learning materials. Many books are even available for free. You may even be reading this book on your phone/tablet right now! Technology has certainly made it easier to access reliable sources of information in a private way. Another option is to make time to listen to one of the many Witchcraft podcasts available, which can add another level to your research and learning.

I've found that morning and evening rituals are easier to build into my routine when they enhance actions and activities I already do, such as visualizing how my face wash and cleanser wash away the accumulated energies of the day, and placing a beauty charm on the moisturizer and face oil I apply before bed. Drinking a cup of chamomile tea or another relaxing herbal blend is part of my nightly routine as it helps me to wind down. Herbal tea bags of all flavors have gradually found their way into non-specialist shops and supermarkets as the years have progressed, and drinking them isn't now considered strange. Make your own herbal teas easily by cutting open the teabags of your choice and using the dried herbs within to create your own blend. You could also put these herbs in a muslin bag and use them in a ritual bath.

Another ritual I like to perform before bed is to cleanse my whole self to make sure I remove any undesirable energies that have accumulated over the course of the day. This is something you can do in the broom closet as there are more ways to cleanse yourself and your space other than burning herbs. Try visualization, light, or sound, all of which can be practiced as subtly as you need them to be but are all still very effective.

WITCHCRAFT
& Self-Care

Self-care is vital for us all, especially in the modern age we live in, and regardless of who we are, we all need to take care of our physical, mental, and spiritual health. Self-care is about more than just facials and bubble baths, and is arguably even more necessary when you are practicing your Craft in the broom closet. Staying in the broom closet is not an easy path to take, and is one that can weigh heavily on your emotional wellbeing, but the practices of Witchcraft themselves can provide a framework that helps us to look after ourselves. Nature-based practices in particular are vital routes for self-care and building small rituals into your daily life can help you ground yourself, lowering levels of stress and anxiety.

Getting out into nature as much as you can is important, whether that's going to your favorite nature spot, getting out into your yard or going to a green space like a public park if you are an urban Witch. The more connection you have with the natural world, the greater the positive impact on your wellbeing will be. Try some gentle exercise such as yoga or meditation outside if you can. If some of these are already part of your daily practice, switching your activities from inside to outside (when the weather allows) can be an easy way to help you

incorporate time in the natural world into your day. Having regular breaks away from technology in today's world is important for us all, so swap some daily screen time with a walk or read that book you've been wanting to start for months.

Learning how to ground yourself properly is an invaluable skill, one that will help to foster a greater sense of wellbeing to help in the practice of your Craft. Sit comfortably and visualize a white light filling the core of your body. Let it flow down toward the ground to meet the Earth's energy. To help, see your own energy as a different color. Visualize the Earth's energy moving to fill your entire body and visualize your own energy mingling with it. If you feel drained, you can pull up more the Earth's energy into yourself and use it to recharge and rebalance yourself.

Starting a self-care journal is a good way to record your thoughts and feelings and all the acts of self-care. Journaling in itself can be a therapeutic action but keeping a track of how different methods of caring for yourself made you feel and how they impacted upon your wider sense of wellbeing means you can see any patterns that emerge. It can help you to understand yourself better and how to give your body and soul what they most need.

WITCHCRAFT AND SELF-CARE

Start a self-care journal.

Learn how to ground yourself properly.

Listen to your body, rest, and slow down when needed.

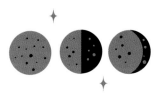

Flow with the moon's cycle. Manifest at the Full Moon, rest in the Waning Crescent.

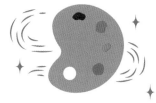

Embrace and feed your creativity.

Write down any negativity you're holding onto. Burn or cut the paper to release.

Cleanse yourself and your space regularly.

Have a break away from technology.

Go outside and connect with nature.

Meditate or practice yoga outside.

Regularly express gratitude.

Eat well, nourish your body.

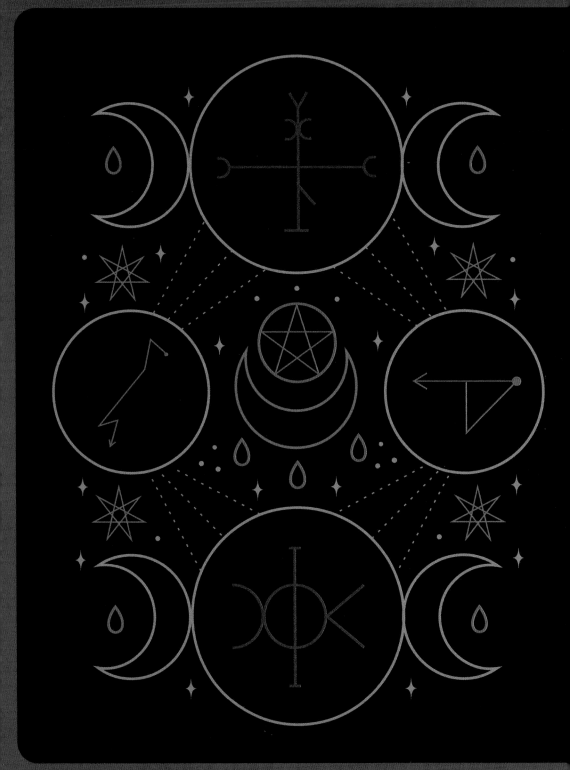

6

SIGILS

A sigil is a magickal sign or symbol that has been created to represent a particular intention or goal. Witches and occultists have used sigils for centuries but symbols for specific purposes such as to honor a deity (in a religious context) have been used by many ancient civilizations stretching back millennia—examples are the Christian cross and the Jewish Star of David.

In modern-day magick, sigils are often used for personal matters such as attracting wealth, protection, healing, setting stronger boundaries, and to represent an intention or thought. Sigils are a great way to give a physical shape to a specific thought or goal. They can be drawn, carved, or burned into any kind of material, but usually they are simply drawn with a pen or pencil on a piece of paper.

USING SIGILS
In Your Craft

Sigil magick is based on the philosophy that we are all the creators of our own future and we all have the potential to bring about the change we want to see in our lives. They can help you manifest the seeds of intention you plant as you create and craft the sigil. It is the action of creation itself that gives a sigil its power. This is one of my favorite kinds of magick because there isn't really right or wrong way to make a sigil. They can be as simple or complex as you want them to be, which makes it an accessible form of magick for those just starting their Witchcraft journey.

As you create your sigil, you weave your creativity, determination, willpower, and ritual into your intentions, which supercharges their magickal ability to manifest your desires. Sigil magick is incredibly empowering as it puts you firmly in the driving seat of your own life.

Intention is a core part of this kind of magick—it's the strength of it that encodes your sigils with the things you want to manifest.

Sigils act as a key to your subconscious mind, which enables you to access your full magickal potential. They are able to move past anything that may be holding you back such as negative thoughts, doubts, fear, and the self-consciousness of your conscious mind. These magickally charged symbols help to reprogram the subconscious mind and help to replace any self-limiting beliefs with focused thoughts about exactly what you want to manifest.

Although sigils are powerful magickal tools, they're not a substitute for action. Sigils can be used to bring about great inner change, but you must also do the outer work too. Combining your sigil magick with action will help to ensure success of your magick.

Sigils can be used in many ways and in many different places. Often, a sigil has to be destroyed in some way to release their magick into the Universe, so it can work on your subconscious (see page 139). Here, I've included an example of the kind of magick that aligns well with each specific place, but it is by no means the only kind of magick connected to each specific physical location.

They can be drawn on yourself with a pen, then washed off, drawn on a rock and then thrown it into the sea or a river to let the water wash the sigil off, and they can even be draw on your food. Use a sauce to draw a sigil on a pizza, salad or sandwich, then eat it. One of my favorites methods is, after a hot bath, to trace a sigil in the condensation on the mirror, then watch it disappear as the condensation fades.

Draw a sigil to help
enforce boundaries on a
chalk or dry board and
then erase it.

Trace a confidence sigil on a
flower to signify your confidence
growing. Harvest a petal or leaf
to release the energy.

DRAWING AND
REMOVING SIGILS

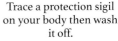

Draw a purification or
banishing sigil on a rock or
a piece of lead, then throw it
into a body of water.

Trace a protection sigil
on your body then wash
it off.

Draw a health sigil on
your food then eat it.

Write a home protection or
house blessing in the
condensation of a window
or mirror, then watch it fade.

CREATING YOUR SIGIL

Intention is central to sigil magick .

When writing your intentions, make sure they aren't too vague or complex. Keep them clear and precise.

Visualize your intentions coming to fruition to help keep them focused.

Once you have created and activated your sigil, try to forget about it.

This helps to commit your sigil to your subconcious, where it can work on what it was created for.

Sigils aren't a replacement for action. You must do the outer work to support the inner work.

CREATING
Your Sigil

When crafting your own sigil, there are five important steps that are necessary to the creation of all kinds of sigil magick:

Consider your Intentions

Before you put pen to paper, it's good to formulate clear and well-defined intentions. If your intentions are too vague, the energy of the sigil will be unfocused and is less likely to be as effective. The same is likely to happen if your intentions are overly complicated. If you have more than one intention, make a sigil for each separate intention to help ensure their aims and goals are sharp.

Phrase your Intentions

Ways to phrase your intentions could include:

I need... "I need strength to overcome the challenges in my life."

I am... "I am protected from any negative energies."

I welcome... "I welcome more love into my life."

Design your sigil

There are many different techniques you can use to design your sigil, such as the the sentence method (see page 136). You can also research and use methods such as the wheel method and the Saturn grid method.

Charge and activate your sigil

Choose how you would like to charge and activate your sigil (see page 139). This step is important, as it gives you the opportunity to pour more power into your sigil, and then control how this power is released.

Forget about it!

Once you've created and activated your sigil, try your best to forget about. This step is often skipped over, but it's an essential step to complete your sigil magick. The act of forgetting the sigil helps to commit your symbol to your subconscious where it can work without being influence and disturbed by your conscious mind and its limitations.

THE
Sentence Method

As the creation process is central to this form of magick, it's probably unsurprising to know that the sigils you make yourself are usually far more powerful than those made by others. This doesn't mean that you can't use a sigil created by someone else if it aligns with what you want to manifest, but because the actual act of creating and crafting the sigil yourself is missing, it can make it less effective.

The sentence method was the first method I was taught to use to design sigils, and I still use it as part of my own practice.

Step One

Decide on the purpose of your sigil and formulate your intentions. This could be anything from attracting prosperity and wealth, to better health, or strength to reinforce your personal boundaries. Remember that the longer the sentence you begin with, the more complicated your sigil will be once it's finished, and more complex doesn't necessarily mean more powerful. Once you're happy, write down your intentions in full as seen on the first line of writing in the example.

Step Two

Next, remove all the vowels and any repeated letters from your sentence. At this point, the aim is to simplify your intentions as much as possible.

Step Three

Deconstruct the remaining letters into simple lines and curves that represents the remaining letters of your intentions. For example, the letter "M" could be broken down into the shapes I V I. The letter "H" can be broken down into I – I.

Step Four

The last step is to use all the simplified lines and curves from step three and construct the shapes into one complete design. You can flip the different lines and curves around and change the positions until you find a design you're happy with—remember it's completely your own choice where you place each separate shape. I chose to make the "I am protected" sigil in the example based on the basic shape of a cross, but this was purely a personal choice. It's a great opportunity to be creative! Just be sure to use all the simplified letters from your intentions in the final design of your sigil.

THE SENTENCE METHOD: EXAMPLE

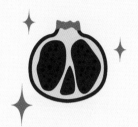

1. I AM PROTECTED

2. X AM PROTECTED

3. I V I I P I P \ C I)

4.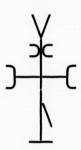

"I am protected"

CREATING YOUR SIGIL

ACTIVE ACTIVATION

Burning the sigil

Let water dissolve the paper

Tear the sigil in half

Draw it on your body and
wash it off

PASSIVE ACTIVATION

Carve sigil into a piece
of wood

Draw a sigil on paper and
keep it with you

Draw a sigil on your body
and let it rub off gradually

Carve a sigil into a candle
and burn when needed

SIGIL
Charging & Activation

Once you have designed your sigil and have drawn it out onto your chosen item, it's time to charge and activate it. These are two crucial parts of any kind of sigil magick so shouldn't be skipped over. It is through the acts of charging and activating your sigil that you concentrate the energies of your intentions and then release them for their magick to work.

Charging

Charging your sigil is the process by which you pour more of your intentions into the symbol to create a sigil of power. We project and receive energy throughout our bodies, but our hands in particular are powerful tools in energy work like this. To find your projective hand, interlock your fingers together, letting your hands rest in your lap or on a table. Look at your thumbs and their position to see which thumb is on top of the other. The thumb on top is your projective hand.

Hold your sigil in your projective hand and focus on the specific intentions you have set. Use visualization to see yourself actualizing the intentions of your sigil and getting to where you want to be. Take your time to feel your energy flowing from your projective hand and into the sigil to charge it. When you feel ready, it's time to activate it.

Activation

Activation is a way of releasing the energy of your sigil into the Universe so it can do its work. There are two types of sigil activation: active and passive. Active activation is great for quick and powerful manifestations, such as banishing something, as the sigil only needs to be used once and will be destroyed in the activation process. Burning is a traditional way to actively activate sigils, but drawing your sigil on anything you can tear up or dissolve in water is a great alternative method.

If you want the magick of your sigil to last and have an effect over a longer period of time, like a sigil for a project you are working on or a sigil to increase something, passive activation is a more suitable method. Using this method means the sigil is not destroyed, but is kept so it can continue to work its magick, and release its energy slowly, helping you to achieve your long-term goals. These sigils can be carved into wood or wax, sewed onto material, drawn on paper, or even on your body, letting it gradually fade. Passively activated sigils can last anything from days to years.

7

HERBS

Herbs have been used for thousands of years in Witchcraft and healing. I have been in love with the magick of herbs since the early days of my practice and the more I grow as a Witch, the more I find myself using them in my Craft. A herb can be defined as any type of plant with leaves, seeds, or flowers that are useful to humans, whether they are used for their flavor in cooking, for healing in the form of medicine, for their fragrance in incense and perfumes, and in our case, for magick.

Herbs embody the four elements. They grow in the soil (Earth), use the light and warmth of the Sun (Fire) to make the nutrients they need, use moisture from the soil and the rain to grow (Water) and take carbon dioxide from their immediate environment to make oxygen (Air). Using herbs in your Craft means you are working with the very elements of nature and the power of the earth's energy in its strongest form.

Before you begin working with herbs, there are some ground rules that you must follow. Never ingest or touch an unidentified herb. Always research your herbs before ingesting or making skin contact with them, and seek advice from a medical herbalist or doctor before before working with any herbs if you are pregnant, suffer from any allergies, or have any health concerns. If you feel unwell or have any reactions to a herb, seek medical advice immediately.

HOW TO USE HERBS

2. Oils
Use olive, sunflower, or grapeseed oil as a base and add your chosen herb and leave to infuse. Use it to dress candles, anoint yourself, and your tools.

3. Ritual baths
Sprinkle appropriate herbs in a hot bath or place the herbs in a cloth bag, then add to your bath. Let the herbs infuse your bath water and bathe with intention.

1. Burning
Many herbs, once fully dried, can be burned on a hot charcoal to release the smoke. Incense sticks and cones are other good alternatives.

4. Tincture
Herbs are added, usually to ethyl alcohol but sometimes in glycerin, to preserve and help extract the goodness. Take 2 tablespoons each day or night.

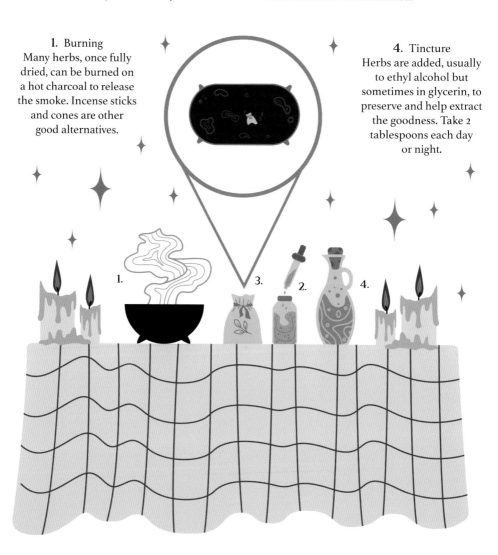

1.

3.

2.

4.

HOW TO
Use Herbs

There are many ways to incorporate herbs into your practice. Below are some of the different ways to use the magickal and medicinal power of herbs in your Craft.

Incense

Making incense from the dried leaves, stems, and flowers of herbs is one of my favorite ways to use herbs in my Craft. Before burning your herbs, grind them all together using a mortar and pestle. Follow a recipe, usually measured in "parts" or create your own blend.

To burn loose incense, light a charcoal disc and leave it for a few minutes to get hot. Place fully dried herbs on top of the charcoal to release their fragrant smoke. If you prefer, incense sticks and cones are other good options.

Oils

Making a magickal oil using herbs or spices is a simple process. Use grapeseed, olive, or sunflower oil for the base and then add your chosen herbs. Leave for a few weeks to allow the herbs to infuse the oil before using to anoint yourself, candles, other people, or your tools, depending on the properties of the herbs .

You can also use essential oil in place of dried herbs if you prefer. Oils, made either way, generally have a shelf life of two to three years.

Ritual baths

Herbs can be sprinkled directly into a hot bath or can be placed in a small cloth bag and used like a teabag to infuse your bath water. Using a bag means you can still benefit from the magickal properties of the herbs, but the herbs won't clog up your drain. Prepare and enjoy your bath with the intention of your magick in mind. **Caution:** If you have sensitive skin which is prone to allergic reactions, always perform a patch test with an infusion or decoction of the herb(s) you want to use in your ritual bath first.

Pouches/sachets

Herbs can be placed in a small bag so you can carry their magick with you. The colored bags jewelry is often packaged in is perfect for this kind of working and these small bags can also be bought inexpensively online in a variety of colors. Chose a colored pouch that aligns with your intentions for a boost of energy.

HOW TO USE HERBS

2. Pouch/Sachet
Spell pouches are easy to make. Place your chosen herbs (and crystals and other items) in a small cotton or jewlery bag and carry it with you.

3. Tea
Herbs can be used in tea. Add dried herbs to a tea strainer and leave to brew in hot water for about 5 minutes before drinking.

1. Decoction
A decoction is a very concentrated infusion made by simmering herbs in water for 20-40 minutes. Tougher parts of herbs and plants are used like bark, roats and seeds.

4. Infusion
An infusion is made by pouring hot water on to herbs to make a tea. Infusions use more herbs and are steeped for longer, usually overnight.

Tea

Also called a tisane, herbal tea has many magickal and health benefits. Gently crush the herbs to help release their flavor and place them in teapot or use in a tea infuser. Pour hot water over the herbs and leave to steep for around five minutes before drinking so the heat of the water can extract their medicinal and magickal benefits.

Infusion

A herbal infusion is made in the same way as an herbal tea but herbs are steeped for much longer to bring out the fuller, deeper flavor of the herbal matter you use. Pour very hot water on safe herbs, dried fruits, leaves, flowers, or seeds to release the flavor. Infusions can be made on the stove by adding your herbs to a pot of gently simmering water. Keep stirring the mixture to release the flavor and the magickal and medicinal properties of your chosen herbs. Cover the pot and let the infusion steep overnight. When making an herbal infusion, more herbs are used than when making an herbal tea. I use roughly 2 to 3 tablespoons of herbs for every average mug of water used. This method favors using safe leaves, stems, and flowers and softer parts of herbs. Strain the herbs before serving. Infusions are best refrigerated and used either as a drink or in your workings within 24 hours.

Decoction

A decoction is a very strong infusion. It is made by boiling herbs in water for an extended period of time to create a concentrated water. This method favors using safe bark, roots, seeds, and the tougher parts of herbs and plants. Use 1 to 2 tablespoons of herbs for 1 cup of cold water, adding more water as required to keep the original level in the pan. Place the water and herbs in a pot and bring to a boil, then simmer for 20-40 minutes. Remove from the heat and leave to cool at room temperature before straining the herbs. A decoction is best used straight away but you can refrigerate any left-overs and use within 48 hours. If you plan to ingest or make skin contact with your decocation, you MUST ensure you use safe ingredients.

Tincture

Tinctures are concentrated herbal extracts made with alcohol or vinegar, taken for their magickal and medicinal properties. The alcohol acts as a solvent that draws out the magickal and medicinal properties of the herbs. Tinctures can be taken straight or diluted in water or tea. Place your herbs in a bottle (fill it half full of herbs) then fill with vodka that is at least 40% alcohol, or with vinegar. Leave the mixture to extract for around 8 weeks before use. Herbal tinctures made with alcohol or vinegar have a shelf life of 3–5 years as the alcohol preserves the mixture.

EVERYDAY HERBS
AND SPICES

1. Basil—Protection, home protection, love, lust, psychic abilities, wealth
2. Bay Laurel—Protection, purification, success, psychic abilities, wishes, prosperity
3. Black pepper—Protection, courage, banish negativity or jealousy, stimulate memory
4. Cinnamon—Psychic abilities, power, protection, success, lust, money drawing, stregth, spirituality
5. Chamomile—Healing, happiness, calming, sleep, money, love, purification, protection
6. Clove—Protection, money, love, prosperity, exorcism

EVERYDAY *herbs*

BASIL *(Ocimum basilicum)*

Place a sachet of basil in each room of your property to keep away evil or negative energies. Eating basil can summon clarity and inner strength, and placing it in your pockets will help to attract wealth.

BAY LAUREL *(Laurus nobilis)*

Wear a bay leaf as an amulet for protection or cook the leaves in a soup to ward off any negative energy. It is said that if you write a wish on a bay leaf then burn it, you wish will come true. Bay can be used in a ritual bath or in money spells to attract prosperity. Please see ritual baths caution on page 143 before working with this herb if you are prone to allergic reactions.

BLACK PEPPER *(Piper nigrum)*

When mixed with salt, black pepper can be sprinkled along the threshold of your home for protection or to drive away any negative or unwanted energies. Carrying black peppercorns as a charm can ward off jealousy.

CINNAMON *(Cinnamomum zeyanicum)*

Burning cinnamon inside as incense can raise the spiritual vibrations of a room. It can also be used in money drawing and prosperity spells and to increase your natural psychic abilities. Cinnamon will also give any spell work an extra boost of power.

CHAMOMILE *(Chamaemelum nobile)*

Chamomile has incredible healing and calming powers. Drink in a tea to help relieve stress, promote inner peace, and aid sleep. Burn the flower as incense for purification, or use for personal protection by taking a ritual bath with ground up chamomile. Generally speaking chamomile is helpful for allergies, but some people are allergic/sensitive to it. If you have sensitive, reactive skin, it's a good idea to try a little chamomile infusion on your hands before taking a full bath in it.

CLOVE *(Eugenia carophyllus)*

When burned as incense it purifies the air and dispels any negative energies. Burning cloves as incense or pushing cloves into a red candle and burning helps to stop gossip and rumors. It's a good ingredient in banishing spells and workings to protect against psychic attacks.

CLOVER *(Trifolium)*

The common three-leaved clover is highly protective, especially if worn as an amulet. The less common four leaved clover strengthens psychic abilities. The rare five leaved clover can draw money, place one in your wallet to attract wealth.

CUMIN *(Cumimum cyminum)*

Cumin promotes fidelity. When burned with frankincense, cumin's protective qualities are enhanced. It's particularly useful for protection against theft. Sprinkle seeds around your home or at the main entrances to your property to ward off thieves.

DILL *(Anethum graveolens)*

Dill is a great ingredient to use in love spells and charms. To attract romance and make yourself irresistible to a lover, place the seeds in a muslin pouch and use it in a ritual bath or hang under your showerhead. Use dill leaves and seeds in wealth spells. Remember to check your sensitivity to dill before taking a bath in it, if you are prone to allergies.

LAVENDER *(Lavendula officinale)*

Burn lavender as incense (loose, sticks or cones) or use in a pouch under your pillow to induce calm and aid sleep. Drinking lavender and chamomile tea before bed combats insomnia. To attract love, place lavender flowers in your closet to fragrance your clothes.

LEMON BALM *(Melissa officinalis)*

Known as *The Elixir of Life*, lemon balm is associated with healing. Soak lemon balm in wine and share it to deepen your bond with your partner or to strengthen a friendship, Burn as incense with lemon grass to cleanse and purify.

MINT *(Mentha spp)*

Associated with the element Air, mint aids communication and adds strength and power to your words, particularly if consumed in a tea. Burning, carrying, and eating mint helps to attract love as well as preserve and protect relationships.

EVERYDAY HERBS
AND SPICES

1. Clover—Protection, money, success, luck, fidelity, love, purification
2. Cumin—Protection, fidelity, prevents theft, peace
3. Dill—Protection, love, lust, money, luck, romance
4. Lavender—Sleep, peace, love, calm, protection, purification, mental clarity
5. Lemon balm—Calm, success, healing, longevity, balance, purification, anxiety
6. Mint—Healing, protection, money, luck, communication, prosperity, cleansing

NUTMEG *(Myristica fragrans)*

Use nutmeg oil to anoint a green candle, roll it in nutmeg powder and burn it to attract money. Do the same to a purple candle to heighten psychic abilities. Add nutmeg to food and drink to enhance divinatory abilities and to encourage clear sight.

OREGANO *(Origanum vulgare)*

Oregano can help to strengthen an existing love but also aid the process of letting go of a loved one following a bereavement or relationship break-up. Dress a candle by rubbing oil into a green candle, then rolling it in dried oregano before burning to attract luck and wealth.

ROSE *(Rosa spp)*

The rose is strongly associated with romance and is traditionally used in love spells. Burn dried petals as incense or drink a tea to increase feelings of passion. Sprinkle dried red rose or a few drops of rose oil in a ritual bath to attract romance and to foster feelings of self-love.

ROSEMARY *(Rosmarinus officinalis)*

This versatile herb improves mental powers and memory. Place rosemary in oil and use to anoint a yellow candle. Burn on a Thursday to help academic study and improve grades. Use rosemary in a ritual bath for personal cleansing or burn for smoke cleansing.

THYME *(Thymus vulgaris)*

Burning thyme with frankincense before a spell or ritual is a great space cleanser and purifier. Make thyme oil to use in a ritual bath for personal cleansing and to renew the spirit. Placed under your pillow, thyme can aid restful sleep and promote good dreams.

YARROW *(Achillea millefolium)*

Yarrow is protective when worn in a magickal pouch/sachet and it also helps to bring the wearer courage. Hold it in your hand for a few minutes to reduce feelings of fear. Brew as tea to increase clairvoyant powers or rub yarrow on your eyelids to raise psychic awareness.

EVERYDAY HERBS
AND SPICES

3. 4.

2. 5.

1. 6.

1. Nutmeg—Luck, money, fidelity, psychic abilities, power, success
2. Oregano—Money, health, love, happiness, peace, courage
3. Rose—Love, romance, healing, love divination
4. Rosemary—Protection, mental powers, purification, healing, love, sleep, blocks negative energy
5. Thyme—Good health, purification, love, healing, psychic ability, sleep
6. Yarrow—Love, courage, psychic ability, exorcism

FORAGING

Foraging is the practice of finding and using tools, food, and medicinal herbs from the natural world.

Foraging knowledge can be applied to Witchcraft and can give a free supply of spell ingredients.

Foraging is a great opportunity to expand your herb knowledge and read about their magickal and medicinal properties.

Foraging regulary is a good way to connect with the changing of seasons and the rhythms and cycles of the earth.

Don't overlook the plants we know as 'weeds'. They have a wide range of magickal properties and are just useful in spellwork as herbs.

You'll probably be surprised about what's growning in your local environment, even in urban areas.

FORAGING

Foraging is the skill and practice of finding food, medicinal herbs, and even tools from the natural world. It's by no means a modern practice and it's usually done by hand and mainly for individual use. Foraging and Witchcraft go hand in hand and the practice can bring so many benefits. It gives us a reason and an opportunity to get out into nature. This helps us to connect with the changing of the seasons and how the passing of time affects the natural world locally. By actively going out to look for useful and identifiable herbs, you begin to find yourself noticing the smaller details of the cycles of the earth at the same time. It can help you connect with Mother Nature on a deeper level as you physically handle her bounty.

Foraging also gives us access to a vast array of spell ingredients, and all for free! It's a practice that is truly available to every Witch, even if you are on a tight budget. Even if you live in an urban area, you might be surprised to find what is growing in your local area. Look in hedgerows, parks, nature spots, woods, forests, and even your yard to get an idea about the kinds of herbs available to you in this way. There is something very special about using the herbs you have foraged yourself in your spells and rituals, particularly if you harvest them with intentions that align with their properties.

Identifying the herbs you find can be tricky but if you're unsure about an herb you find, its best to leave it alone until you know more. Luckily there are many good apps out there that allow you to take a picture of the unidentified herb and it will give you its name and species. If you prefer a book, then Scott Cunningham's *Encyclopaedia of Magical Herbs* is a great foraging companion. The one rule when foraging is to remember to only take what you need and don't over harvest—we have a responsibility to care for the natural world as we practice our Craft. Always ask for a plant's permission before picking from it.

Tarragon

Lemon balm

Mint

Lavender

Basil

Parsley

High-moisture herbs

Low-moisture herbs

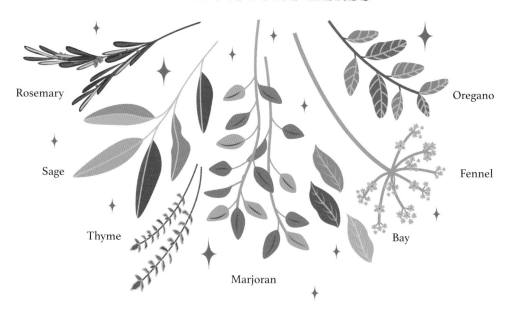

Rosemary

Oregano

Sage

Fennel

Thyme

Bay

Marjoran

DRYING
Herbs

Drying herbs is a fairly easy process and there are two common methods that are simple and don't require any special tools or materials. The drying method you use is usually determined by the moisture content and fragility of the herbs you want to dry. Those herbs with a high moisture content will mold quickly so are best oven dried. Air drying is the method better suited to drying out herbs with a low moisture content. This is a much longer process than oven drying, but these kinds of herbs will not mold before they are fully dried out. Dried herbs are often better than using fresh as the drying out process can concentrate the qualities of the dried herb to make them 3 to 4 times stronger once the water inside them evaporates.

Air Drying

Air drying herbs can be done in bunches or by laying the herbs out flat. If the herbs you want to dry are delicate and fall apart easily when handled, it is best to air dry them flat. Discard any damaged parts then spread out the healthy leaves and stems evenly, in a single layer, on a baking tray lined with a baking sheet. Place them in a shady spot with low humidity. Turn the herbs every 12 hours or so to enable them to dry evenly and fully. This method dried herbs in about 2-4 days.

If your chosen herbs are more robust, you can dry them by placing them on a drying rack or by tying them in bunches. Tie 3-4 stems together with string and hang them upside-down in a dry place. As the herbs dry and shrink, you might need to tighten the string. The process takes 2 to 4 weeks.

Oven Drying

Spread the herbs out evenly, in a single layer, on a baking tray lined with baking paper. Place your herbs in a preheated oven, set to the lowest possible temperature, and leave for 2 to 4 hours. Keep an eye on them as herbs are burned easily. If you're worried about your herbs burning but still want to oven dry them, there's the option to leave the door open a little to allow air to circulate.

HERBS &
The Moon

There's no doubt that the Moon plays an important part in so many aspects of Witchcraft, and harvesting herbs is no exception. The energy of herbs and plants flows with the lunar phases just as the tides are affected by the gravitational pull of the Moon at different stages of her cycle. Some Witches choose to follow these cycles to guide them as to when to harvest the herbs they need to give their workings a boost on energy.

There is a strong tradition in folklore that the vitality of all herbs, particularly their flowers, leaves, and seeds is enhanced and concentrated by the Waxing or Full Moon as it draws up energy from the Earth into the tips of the herbs, much like the pull of the Moon on the tides. When the Moon is Waning or New, this energy shrinks back down towards the Earth, making this the best time to harvest the roots of herbs or plants for use in magickal workings.

Conscious harvesting uses the Moon as a guideline for when to harvest herbs, but you can also align gathering your herbs to the day of the week and the time of day that best aligns with the intention of your workings and the intentions of the herbs themselves. See page 96 for details about the magickal significance of the days of the week and the times of the day to help you choose the right time for harvesting your herbs.

Using the Moon cycle to determine when to harvest herbs isn't a practice you must use in your Craft if it doesn't resonate with you. It's not something you should feel pressured to incorporate. I often use this practice when I can plan my workings well in advance, but sometimes we can all find ourselves in a pinch and we don't have the luxury of time to either plan or wait for the necessary Moon phase to come around. Many Witches, myself included, use herbs that have been harvested and dried by someone else where there is no way to know what Moon phase they were gathered on. Don't worry that this might have a negative impact on your spell work. There's no doubt that conscious harvesting adds energy to your workings but using herbs that haven't been gathered this way will certainly not make your spell work ineffective or fail.

The phases of the Moon can be used to know when it's best to harvest herbs

This won't make your workings fail or make the herbs ineffective, they just won't be as powerful as they could be

During the Waxing and Full Moon, the moon's gravitational pull draws the Earth's energy into the leaves, flowers and seeds, making it the best time to harvest them

HERBS AND THE MOON

If this method doesn't resonate with your craft, don't feel pressured to incorporate it into your practice. Do what feels right for you

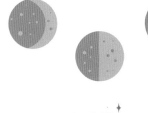

During the Waning and New Moon, this energy returns towards the Earth. This a good time to harvest roots

Harvesting herbs based on the day of the week as well as the phase of the Moon gives your magick a boost of energy

YES

YES

NO

NO

8

DIVINATION

Divination is the art of gaining hidden knowledge or foretelling the future through the use of interpretive tools. This knowledge may come from the divine, from your own intuitive senses, or from your subconscious, but if you can tap into it, you can use it as a key to access you higher self and provide the answer you are searching for. Usually, divination offers guidance rather than specific answers and it's up to us to interpret this guidance by using a divinatory tool such as tarot, a pendulum, or scrying.

Many Witches choose to practice divination as part of their Craft. It's common for a Witch to practice more than one form of divination within their Craft, but if you don't feel attracted to any kind of divination, don't feel pressured to do so. It certainly doesn't make you any less of a Witch!

Divination comes in many different forms and no one method is better or more valid than the others. A method is usually based on your personal preference and which divination tool speaks to you the most. Take your time to look at the different types of divination and use your intuition to see which calls to you!

KING
Leadership, authority, controlling, maturity, stepping up, decisive, domineering

QUEEN
Nurturing, grounding, receptive, subtle control, draws energy from within, caregiver, love

COURT CARDS

KNIGHT
Adventure, progression, working towards a goal, prone to excess, act first before thinking

PAGE
Childlike, newness, curious, beginnings, spontaneous, initiation, exploring new things, start of a journey, potential

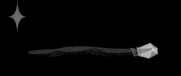

WANDS
FIRE
Inspiration, enthusiasm, energy, goals, the mind, ambitions, dreams

SWORDS
AIR
Action, intelligence, communication, thoughts, truth

TAROT SUITS

PENTACLES
EARTH
Material possessions, wealth, home, generosity, money

CUPS
WATER
Emotions, intuition, creativity, quality of your relationship, love , friendship

TAROT
(Cartomancy)

This is the first type of divination that I ever tried, and it remains my favorite many years later! Tarot cards are incredible healing tools—they help us to access our true feelings and understand ourselves on a deeper, soul level. It's a common misconception that tarot cards foretell the future, but they don't work this way. Instead, they give spiritual guidance and help you connect with your own inner wisdom to give you a deeper understanding about your circumstances.

A tarot deck is made up of 78 cards, each with their own meaning and symbolism. Each deck is split into two parts, the Major Arcana and the Minor Arcana.

The Major Arcana

There are 22 cards in the Major Arcana, and they represent the big life lessons we experience as we move through life. These cards speak about long term, and often karmic and spiritual lessons that influence life. The complete Major Arcana tells the story of a journey, with each card having a deep soul meaning of its own. The Fool (the first card in the Major Arcana) is the main figure in this journey and the remaining 21 cards tell of his life at various stages as he grows, learns, suffers setbacks, and faces challenges. His journey reflects our own and the big themes in life that we all experience as we move through our own

life journey so are considered to be the foundation of each tarot deck.

The Minor Arcana

There are 56 cards in the Minor Arcana and they are arranged into four suits—Wands, Swords, Pentacles, and Cups. Where the Major Arcana represents long-term influences, the cards of the Minor Arcana usually have a short and temporary effect. They highlight the energy that's currently moving through your life and they offer insight into your present situation. The guidance they give isn't set in stone and you have the ability to change your situation if you don't like what the cards show. You are in complete control and the Minor Arcana cards can help you find what action to take within your current situation in order to manifest your goals. Within the Minor Arcana there are the 16 Court Cards—Kings, Queens, Knights, and Pages. In tarot readings, they mostly represent a person (whether that be yourself or someone else) and the life stages from child to highly skilled adult. From this, each card has their own set of characteristics and personality traits. They can help us to understand others and ourselves on a deeper level as the Court Cards can give us an insight into what the person in question thinks, feels, and why they act the way they do.

1. *New beginnings, purity, potential, opportunity*

2. *Balance, duality, choices, partnership, union*

3. *Growth, creativity, groups, team building, competition*

4. *Structure, manifestation, foundations, stability*

5. *Conflict, change, instability, unforeseen obstacles*

6. *Relief from conflict, co-operation, communication*

7. *Reflection, re-evaluation, assessment, self-awareness*

8. *Action, progress, mastery, accomplishments, growth*

9. *Fulfilment, pause, fruition, attainment*

10. *Completion, end of cycle, renewal, rebirth*

READING
Tarot Cards

Starting your tarot journey can feel overwhelming, but you don't have to memorize all 78 cards. There's definitely an easier way! A good method to learn the basics of the Minor and Major Arcana is by using numerology. Using this method, you only need to remember the general meanings of numbers from 1 to 10. Each of the four suits in the Minor Arcana, excluding the Court cards, are numbered between 1 and 10, so learning the meaning of each number can help you get to grips with 40 cards! This can start to build a really solid foundation on which you can build up your tarot knowledge.

Once you have mastered the meanings of the cards numbered 1 to 10, it's also helpful to know more about the four different suits so that you know in what context to place the tarot meanings associated with the numbered cards. See more about Pentacles, Swords, Wands, and Cups on page 160. Combine what you know about the numbers with what you've learnt about the characteristics of each suit and this will give you a working knowledge of each of the 40 Minor Arcana cards.

The numerology method can also be applied to the Major Arcana too. Although there are 22 cards in the Major Arcana, it's really easy to apply the numerology method. For the cards numbered 1 to 10, use the meanings for the numbers shown opposite. For those cards numbered 11 to 22, simply take the two single digits of each card and add them together to get a number between 1 and 10. For example, The Hanged Man, card number 12, is 1+2 = 3, and the number three represents creativity and growth.

Although the numerology method can't be applied to the Court cards, there is still an easy way to interpret them. Most often, these cards represent a person—understanding the different personality traits and characteristics associated with Kings, Queens, Knights, and Pages can help you to interpret their meaning. These meanings can then be placed into the context of which suit they are to help build up an understanding of each card. This method makes learning tarot much more accessible and less overwhelming. It gives you working knowledge that you can use as a base that you can build on as your practice and learn more.

TAROT &
Playing Cards

You can use an ordinary pack of playing cards as a tarot deck. This is a great option if you are in the broom closet and don't have the option to own tarot cards. Many homes have a deck of playing cards laying around in a drawer or they are inexpensive to buy, and can be used as a low-key way to practice divination. In this section, I will talk about how to do this.

Although the widespread use of tarot cards as a form of divination didn't take off until the late 1700s, tarot was first designed as a card game in medieval Europe, particularly in Italy. Known as trionfi, this popular game contained cards with four suits and court cards, which we now know as the Minor Arcana. The crucial difference is a deck of playing cards is made up of 52 cards, whereas a tarot deck has 78 cards. A deck of playing cards is therefore missing the 22 cards of the Major Arcana and while this could mean the extra depth and meaning these cards bring will be missing, it doesn't mean that divination using playing cards can't provide a detailed reading.

Playing cards can often be a little harder to read because there are no images to guide you and give you hints as to what the cards mean like you would with traditional tarot cards. The four different suits of the playing cards correspond to the four traditional suits of a tarot deck:

SPADES–SWORDS (Air)
HEARTS–CUPS (Water)
DIAMONDS–PENTACLES (Earth)
CLUBS–WANDS (Fire)

Once you know which suit corresponds to which, you can then apply the numerology method outlined in the last section. Each playing card is numbered and corresponds to the same numerological tarot meanings with the Aces being number one. The same can be done for the court cards in the deck of playing cards, using the same meanings for the Kings and Queens, but in a deck, the Pages and Knights are replaced with a Jack. This card is a mixture of the characteristics of the Knight and the Page together—a rebel, risk taker, someone who falls in love too easily, has hidden depths, is a hard worker, and is ambitious. This will give you the foundations you need to work on expanding your knowledge, so you are able to interpret the meaning of all the playing cards as tarot cards.

PENDULUM *Dowsing*

A pendulum is a small weight suspended on the end of a piece of cord or chain. When it is held so the pendulum dangles down, a question can be asked and the way the weight moves provides an answer. A pendulum is often a crystal on a length of chain, but you can make your own if you prefer. I use a pendulum made from a small silver Pentacle pendant and a necklace my parents bought me when I first began my Witchcraft journey. A pendulum can even be as simple as a needle stuck in a cork, hanging from a piece of thread.

Pendulum dowsing helps you to tap into your subconscious mind and it uses your higher guidance to answer your questions. The information you receive is coming from you, and the pendulum acts as transmitter of the answers it picks up from your subconscious. The unconscious mind is very receptive and is open to receiving intuitive messages. Usually, our conscious mind acts as a filter and makes it harder for these messages to come through, but pendulum dowsing bypasses the conscious mind and taps into the subconscious, where information can come forward. This form of divination is best suited to questions that have a "yes", "no", or "maybe" answers.

Before you begin, it's a good idea to cleanse your pendulum so that any unwanted energies

attached to it can be removed as they could have an impact on the accuracy of your pendulum. I like to burn rosemary and use visualization, but use whatever method feels right to you.

Find somewhere comfortable to sit and rest your elbow on a solid surface to stabilize your hand. Pinch the chain or string of your pendulum between the thumb and forefinger of your projective hand (see page 139 for how to find your projective hand). Hover the pendulum over a pendulum board or ask the pendulum which movement it wants to use for "yes", "no", and "maybe". When you are trying to read something, like someone's energy or the energy of a specific situation, you might get a better response using your receptive hand (your non-projective hand). This way you can receive the energy rather than pushing it away, so you are able to understand it better.

Now is the time to ask your questions. Take your time and give the pendulum chance to respond. Don't worry if you find it difficult to differentiate between the "yes" and "no" answers at first. The more practice you get, the more definite your pendulum movements tend to be. If you're not sure what the pendulum means, rephrase the question until you get a solid answer. Using a pendulum is an accessible and great discreet form of divination.

SCRYING

Scrying is an ancient form of divination where we gaze into a smooth reflective surface and use our second sight to interpret the messages, guidance or visions we receive. Our second sight is our capacity to see and pick up on the things that can't usually be perceived through our usual five senses. The word "scrying" comes from the Old English word descry, which translates as "to make out dimly". Scrying is therefore about revealing the unseen and unknown. As with other forms of divination, it's not about seeing into the future, it is about crossing over to another level of consciousness where the scryer can access their higher self to find the answers they are looking for.

Scrying is often associated with the crystal ball, but there are many ways to scry. Although they all make use of a different reflective surfaces, how to prepare is the same for all.

When you first begin your scrying practice, you might struggle to "see". Different things work for different people, so try the scrying method that speaks to you the most. It's certainly a learned practice, even if you have a particular gift for this type of divination. There is no right or wrong way to interpret the visions and signs you see, so try to relax and don't worry that you are doing it wrong!

When scrying, turn off the lights and light a few candles to make the perfect darkened atmosphere. Before you begin, it's good to try and relax. Meditation can be helpful as can burning incense like frankincense, patchouli, or mugwort to create the right environment. Make sure your eyes are relaxed, so you are not concentrating too hard as this will help you be open to the images as they come to you. Don't worry if your mind starts to wander, just be sure to keep your eyes fixed softly on the reflective surface. Hold the intention you have chosen as you gaze, which could be anything from achieving a goal, tapping into your psychic abilities, or guidance on a certain situation. Let your eyes soften as you stare and let your body and face reach a deeper sense of relaxation. You are a passive observer who watches the images come and go, and as they do, you interpret them. It's common for images to only begin to reveal themselves after 10-15 minutes of gazing if you are new to the practice. Patience is truly the key, but it will certainly be worth it!

CRYSTAL BALL
Crystallomancy
A crystal ball is used as a reflective surface. Light candles to provide shadows and light.

SMOKE
Capnomancy
Create smoke from fire or incense and interpret the shape it makes.

MIRROR
Catoptromancy
A normal mirror or a special black scrying mirror can be used as a reflective surface.

SCRYING METHODS

FIRE
Pyromancy
Gaze into a flame as the reflective surface. The shapes of the flames can be interpreted.

WAX
Carromancy
Fill a bowl with water then drop candle wax onto the surface of the water.

WATER
Hydromancy
Use a bowl full of water as the reflective surface (black food coloring optional).

TEA LEAF READING
(Tasseography)

Tea leaf reading is an ancient form of divination that first began in China where tea drinkers would interpret the different shapes that their tea leaves left in the bottom of their cups. Tasseography, where coffee grounds or wine sediment is used as well as tea leaves, also has origins in the Middle East and ancient Greece. The beauty of this form of divination is it doesn't require expensive or unusual tools, so it's not only a thrifty form of divination but is also a discreet one, so could be used in your practice if you are in the broom closet.

It is better to use coarse, loose-leaf tea with a broad leaf as the pieces are bigger and can stick to the side and bottom of the cup better. The tea from a tea bag can be used, but it's not ideal as the pieces of tea are too small and tend to clump together rather than make any discernible shapes. It's traditional to use a teacup and saucer. Teacups have wider rims and sides that slant gently toward the bottom. The shape of a teacup makes it easier for the tea leaves to form a range of different shapes and lines. Many mugs have vertical sides, so the lea leaves tend to run to the bottom rather than stick to the sides.

To make your tea, pour hot water into a cup with a spoonful of tea. Don't add anything else like milk or sugar. You can make tea in a teapot if your prefere, but remember not to use a strainer. As you drink it, meditate on a question or general area of inquiry, keeping your intentions at the forefront of your mind. When you have about half a teaspoon of tea left, swirl the cup around three times in a clockwise direction then place the saucer upside down on top of the cup. Next, flip the cup and saucer upside down to allow the remaining water to drain away into the saucer. Wait for a few moments and, when you feel the time is right, turn the cup the right way and look at the patterns the leaves have made.

When it comes to interpreting tea leaves, there are some traditional meanings to the shapes that form, but this form of divination asks you to let your intuition lead the way. Take note of your first impressions and gut feelings as you look at the shapes of the leaves. Tea leaves that are close to the rim can be interpreted as relating to events in the near future, whereas the leaves on the bottom of the cup relate to events in the far future. This form of divination is perfect for helping you to get in touch with and build your intuitive skills.

CONCLUSION

It is my hope that this book has helped to inspire your Craft, whether you are just starting out on your Witchcraft journey or whether you've been traveling on this path for some time. Magick is an incredible form of nourishment for our wellbeing as it helps us to connect with ourselves and the natural world in a deep and profound way. Nature has the power to ground and center and I truly hope this book has inspired you to incorporate more natural magick into your practice. Remember your journey is your own and following your sense of intuition is the best guide you can have.

FURTHER READING

Margot Adler, Drawing Down the Moon

Diane Ahlquist, Moon Spells

Deborah Blake, Everyday Witchcraft

Raymond Buckland, Complete Books of Witchcraft

Laurie Cabot, Power of the Witch

Scott Cunningham, Wicca: The Guide for the Solitary Practitioner

Scott Cunningham, The Encyclopaedia of Magickal Herbs

Scott Cunningham, Divination for Beginners

Scott Cunningham, Living Wicca

Liz Dean, The Divination Handbook

Gail Duff, The Wheel of the Wiccan Year

Bridget Esselmont, The Ultimate Guide to Tarot Card Meanings

U. D Frater, Practical Sigil Magick

Gemma Gary, A Cornish Book of Ways

Gemma Gary, The Black Toad

Marian Green, A Witch Alone

Elen Hawke, In the Circle; Crafting a Witch's Path

Arin Murphy Hiscock, The Green Witch

Arin Murphy Hiscock, The Witch's Book of Self-Care

D. E. Luet, A Witch's Book of Shadows

Edain McCoy, Sabbats: A Witch's Approach to Living the Old Ways

Nigel G. Pearson, Wortcunning: A Folk Magick Herbal

Nigel G. Pearson, Walking the Tides; Seasonal Rhythms and Traditional Core in Natural Craft

Lidia Pradas, The Complete Grimoire

Doreen Valiente, Where Witchcraft Lives

Joanna Martine Woolfolk, The Only Astrology Book You'll Ever Need

INDEX

Acknowledgments

To all who have supported and walked with me along my journey this far, I am thankful beyond words. You have made this all possible.